1.26.85

Though there is
no better horse than
Peaceful Pal. Love,
Jackie

The Better Horse

Breeding and Training for Equestrian Sports

Jane Kidd

ARCO PUBLISHING, INC.
New York

Published by Arco Publishing, Inc.
215 Park Avenue South, New York, NY 10003

Library of Congress Catalog Card Number: 84-70188

Harness Racing chapter translated by Anders Wallin
Photographs by Kit Houghton; Western riding:
    Amanda Lorraine, *Performance Horseman*
Illustrations by Gisela Holstein
Designed by Neil H. Clitheroe

Printed in Holland

CONTENTS

PREFACE

This has been a fascinating book to put together. From the first I intended to call on the leading authorities and at this level only two – Julian Hipwood and Ragnar Thorngren – had the time or inclination to settle down and write themselves about their methods of improving their horses. Sandra Rappaport in the United States collected her data from leading western trainers, and I had the intriguing task of interviewing the top people in racing, jumping, dressage, eventing and driving. This gave me the opportunity to compare different approaches in the particular sports, and I found that there was a great deal that each activity could learn from the other.

I am grateful to my interviewees, who exposed so much about their successful methods; to Anders Wallin for translating the contribution by the Swedish Harness Racing champion, Ragnar Thorngren; and to our photographer, Kit Houghton, and illustrator, Gisela Holstein, who both took such trouble to show pictorially how we change the natural horse into the high powered athlete necessary for success in today's fast growing equestrian sports.

JANE KIDD

The publishers gratefully acknowledge the generous support of Modern Alarms Ltd. for the production of this book.

CONTRIBUTORS

CAROLINE BRADLEY was a regular member of the British Show Jumping team from 1967 until her tragic death in 1983. She won team gold medals at the 1978 World Championships and 1979 European Championships and was runner up for the Ladies World title in 1974. She was twice a winner of the Queen Elizabeth II Cup.

JULIAN HIPWOOD is Britain's polo captain and at nine goals is one of the highest handicapped players in the world. He has been a member of the winning team at the World Cup in Florida for three years running, from 1981 to 1983.

DAVID HUNT is the leading British dressage trainer. He is also a successful rider, having competed internationally for nearly ten years.

RICHARD MEADE has been the mainstay of the British Event team for twenty years. He has three Olympic gold medals to his credit, two as a team member and one in 1972 as the individual victor.

PETER MUNT started work as a film stunt man. He turned to the slightly more sedate activity of combined driving when it began to take off as an international sport in the 1970s. He first drove internationally in 1980 and became a team member at the World Championships in 1981.

SANDRA RAPPAPORT compiled the chapter on western riding as a result of interviews with such leading figures as Bob Anthony, champion reining trainer and exhibitor; Cal Cooper, trainer and exhibitor of cutting and reining horses; Al Dunning, trainer; Patty Knudson, trail; Doug Lilly, western pleasure; Jerry Wells, conformation; Carol Harris Parker and Jody Galyean, halter and saddle breaking; and Clark Bradley, Riding Program Director at Findlay College, Ohio.

MICHAEL STOUTE is one of Britain's leading flatrace trainers. He has been responsible for a number of classic winners, the most famous of which was the ill-fated British Derby winner, Shergar.

RAGNAR THORNGREN has trained and driven trotters in Hamburg, at the Hanover Shoe Farm in the United States, and in his native Sweden. He has won the Swedish Trotting Derby and the Swedish Championship and has the astonishing total of 1,257 wins to his credit.

CHANGES THROUGH BREEDING

For more than three thousand years people have devoted considerable intellect and skill and large sums of money to changing horses through breeding and training. Adjusting a living creature, balancing how much can be changed without destroying its natural talents, is a fascinating occupation.

The natural horse roamed wild, but was unique amongst its fellow animals which still lead such an existence because it had the intelligence to learn, the temperament which enabled it to be taught, and a physique which could be used to provide man with strength, speed and agility. Horses were first used in about 1750 BC. The power they provided was limited, however, for the ancestors of today's horses were small ponies, not large enough to be ridden and only able to pull chariots in twos and threes. But over the years, through controlled breeding, they were changed into horses which could be galloped into battle, dashingly ridden in displays and sports, or used for pulling various forms of transport. Some were made heavier and stronger to carry heavily armoured knights, to work the land and turn the wheel which gave power to industry. Others were made lighter and faster to provide a speedy means of transport, of mounted attack and of hunting.

Today the motor engine has led to the demise of the horse as an instrument of war and as a source of power for industry, agriculture and transport. Instead it is the athletic ability of the horses in specialized fields which is so highly valued. Thus in recent years the cavalry chargers, carriage horses, industrial and agricultural horses have been changed into lighter, more athletic horses aimed at excelling in a particular sphere of an equestrian sport.

Breeding a champion, whether for racing, show jumping, harness racing or dressage, is today the aim of more and more people. The following pages examine the breeds and types used for the major equestrian sports, how these breeds were developed, what changes had to be made to their ancestors, and what changes are still being made to them to produce horses with the greatest possible natural talent.

PRINCIPLES OF BREEDING

The horses used for each of the sports considered in this book have been changed by selective breeding. Some have become recognized breeds – the thoroughbred is the prime example – others are still being developed in an attempt to find a type which is superior to others for a particular sport.

The changing of horses through breeding is achieved by the use of scientific principles. Clarification of the aims of the breeder is therefore the first stage; once he has specified the talents required he can begin to look for parents which will provide them. In order to develop the desired combination of talents, parents with complementary qualities must be found: one parent might provide the speed, for example, the other the substance.

Cross-breeding

In sports for which a breed of horse has been specifically developed, such as racing and the thoroughbred, both parents may be of the same breed. But in the newer equestrian sports for which no breed has yet been established which is superior to all others, there is a good deal of cross-breeding. This involves putting together different breeds (horses of known ancestry registered in a stud book) or even types (horses which have no pedigrees and are not registered in a stud book, but have similar features, for example hunters or polo ponies).

With such cross-breeding there is always the danger that unwanted characteristics may be reproduced. It is important therefore to breed from stock in which the genes are a relatively known quantity (that is where past generations can be traced and analysed through pedigrees) and to look for prepotent parents: a stallion which 'stamps its stock' to produce consistently progeny with its good features, and a mare which does similarly.

Another danger in cross-breeding is that of breeding from extremes. The horse is a living creature and adjustments can be made only gradually, otherwise the harmony of its make and shape is easily lost. Thus if one parent is a small thoroughbred providing class, speed and elegance and more strength and substance is to be added, it is inadvisable to put it with one of the breeds of heavy horse, as the result might be a heavy-bodied animal on small spindly legs. The heavy horse might be used for the second cross but the first should be with a mid-way breed, such as a carriage horse. Careful calculations are needed and often it will only be in the second or third generation that the required animal is bred.

Line-breeding, in-breeding and out-crossing

Once a suitable animal is bred the aim is to consolidate this type and the talents which it shows. A knowledge of genetics is particularly helpful here, for the aim is to have as high a concentration as possible of the genes for those talents. This is best achieved by using related parents with the required genes (in-breeding), the method allegedly used by the nomadic Arabs to develop the Arab horse. The problem with in-breeding is the frequent adverse effect that it has upon temperament; in the case of spirited thoroughbreds it is likely to make them excessively highly strung. For these, line-breeding is advisable, which is the mating of more distant relatives such as great- or great-great-grandchildren.

With both line-breeding and in-breeding there should be some out-crossing, that is the use of unrelated parents but of the same type or breed. This introduction of alien blood will restore vigour and robustness.

Data required

To be able successfully to use breeding to change horses or to establish a type it is necessary to ascertain as much as possible about the parents. The soundness, conformation, temperament and action of both the stallion and the mare should be thoroughly examined. A performance record is also a great asset, and in this lies the main reason for the success in breeding racehorses compared with those for the newer equestrian sports: the horses have had to prove themselves on the course.

The parents alone can sometimes provide misleading information. A small stallion, for example, may produce large foals, and such a horse might have been rejected for stud work if the pedigree had not been examined and shown that the ancestors were all good-sized animals. The information that can be gained from a pedigree on the soundness, conformation, action, temperament and performance of previous generations is therefore of great relevance in the complementary or consolidatory selection of parents.

The most reliable information, however, comes from the progeny. Examination of the offspring and their records provides the best clue of all to selective breeders, but obviously this can only be ascertained after the parents have been at stud for a number of years.

Thus the principles of selective breeding are a thorough examination of the qualities and performance of breeding stock and their ancestors, and the intelligent use of this information to determine a mating based on cross-breeding, out-crossing, line-breeding or in-breeding according to how near the horse is to the desired type.

Environmental factors

The principles applied to breeding must take into account the influences of the environment. In the natural evolution of the horse, environment has been the major factor. Horses adapted to their habitat by growing thick coats in cold climates (the Shetland pony, for example) and fine ones (like the Arab) where it was hot; by becoming fast and robust if they grazed on plains, the home of the ancestors of today's light horses, but slower, larger and stronger if they inhabited the forests, home of the ancestors of the heavy horses.

When horses are domesticated and protected from gruelling conditions they become less tough, their coats get finer and they grow taller. In short they become more refined. If they are fed the best possible food with beneficial quantities of minerals, their bone tends to grow longer and bigger, their shape larger and better formed. To a certain extent such food can be supplied scientifically, but no substitute has yet been found for good grassland (with plenty of limestone) and a temperate climate during the horses' early years of growth. Thus there are certain established areas of the world where horses tend to grow up healthier and larger; probably the best known of these are Normandy in France, Ireland, Kentucky in the United States, and New Zealand.

The horse's character will also be influenced in these formative years, helping to make it timid or bold, nervous or confident, wild or cooperative. Early encounters with man and other horses can improve or spoil a horse.

Environmental factors therefore influence the horse's size, constitution and attitude, and are important factors to bear in mind when using breeding to change horses.

THE RACEHORSE

Breed: The thoroughbred

The most dramatic changes ever achieved through breeding horses were those made to Britain's racehorses in the late seventeenth and eighteenth centuries. At the beginning of this period the racehorse was the Galloway pony, a tough little animal of about 13 hh; by the end Britain could boast of having established the thoroughbred, the fastest and most expensive breed in the world.

There is little information about how the early stages of this change were made. It is known that in the century following the Restoration of the racing-mad king, Charles II, more than 200 Oriental horses (Arab, Barb and Turk) were imported, and that about three-quarters of these were stallions and the rest mares. These were the foundation stock for the thoroughbred. Records prove that very few were raced, so from this we must deduce that they were imported for the sole purpose of improving the British

Oriental horses of Arab and Barb descent galloping in a fantasia, a traditional display. These Oriental breeds are to be found among the ancestors of all the horses used for the sports discussed in this book. Their endurance, toughness and good looks have made them high-class foundation stock.

Members of the Spanish Riding School in a display on their white stallions, the Lipizzaners. This breed of horse was very popular for dressage as practised in the seventeenth, eighteenth and nineteenth centuries but they rarely excel in today's competitions as they lack the freedom required for the extended gaits. They have, however, been used with success in cross-breeding for dressage and driving horses.

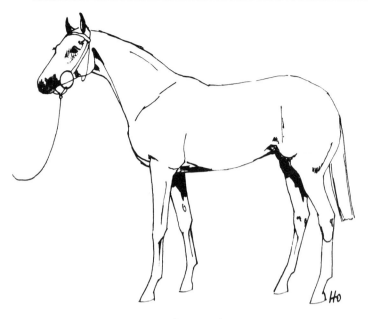

Fig. 1 A good type of yearling racehorse.

racehorse and establishing greater uniformity of type in a hitherto heterogeneous collection of horses.

Of these imports three stallions were to have the greatest influence, and to these three all modern thoroughbreds can be traced. The oldest, the Byerley Turk, was said to have enabled his owner Colonel Byerley to escape in the Battle of the Boyne (1690). In the Byerley Turk's subsequent more peaceful career at stud he was used on a diverse selection of mares in what was then the experimental stage of cross-breeding. There are no authentic records, but his mates are thought to have been the British racing mares in which Galloway, Connemara and Andalusian blood dominated but in which there was an increasing Oriental influence. This cross-breeding period did not last for long, as it is believed that the next great foundation sire, the Darley Arabian, who was imported in 1704, was put to mares of the developing breed.

The last of the great trio to come to England was the Godolphin Arabian, and during the 1720s he was serving mares of a better type so that line-breeding was already being practised.

The British took their breeding of racehorses very seriously. The racecourse was used as a testing ground for all stock (after the early imports) and it was this proving by performance rather than fancy points that was a major factor in the development of a breed which no one has yet been able to improve in terms of speed. Selective methods were rigorously applied and pedigrees were kept, although these were private records until the publication of the first volume of the General Stud Book in 1791.

The speeds of the horses gradually improved. The first great racehorse never to be beaten was Flying Childers (1715), by the Darley Arabian. His great-great-nephew Eclipse (1764) was the second great racehorse. Eclipse was unbeaten in 18 races and was equally successful at stud, being traceable in many of this century's great racehorse's pedigrees.

The end of Eclipse's great career marked the end of an era in racing. This remarkable racehorse competed in races run over distances of 4-12 miles (6-19km), carried weights up to 12 stone (76kg), and sometimes even had to go through heats to reach a final. Only mature, tough horses with great stamina could succeed in such races, and most of them were little more than 14.2 hh. But racing was fast becoming big business, with ever increasing sums of money involved. Breeders needed quicker returns and wanted their horses to run more often. Consequently two-year-old races were started, distances were shortened, weights lightened and the emphasis was switched from endurance to speed.

The breeders' aims now became speed and precocity. Line-breeding helped, as did improved environment (protection, good food, warmth at all times, and so on). The result was that within a hundred years of Eclipse the average height of racehorses had risen by 6 inches (15cm) to 16 hh and their speeds on the racecourse had improved by leaps and bounds. These rapid improvements began to level off from the mid-nineteenth century; the height remained the same, and records were broken less frequently. During the present century times in races have remained almost static: the extraordinary changes that were made to Britain's racehorses in terms of speed, height and precocity have reached a plateau. Despite the input of huge sums of money and man's best brains, the thoroughbred no longer seems capable of improving its speed. Its major sphere for improvement lies in other equestrian fields. Through cross-breeding, the thoroughbred has been and is used to change other types of horses, injecting its unique qualities of 'class', elegance and speed. Thus it has become in its turn one of the chief foundations for other breeds and types used in equestrian sports.

THE HARNESS HORSE

Breeds: American Standardbred, Metis Trotter, French Trotter, Swedish Trotter, German Trotter and Italian Trotter

These are the longest established and best known breeds, but most countries in which harness racing takes place

Fig. 2 A good type of young harness horse.

now organize their own stud books. Although each of these national breeds has some different foundation stock the main lines are thoroughbred and Norfolk Trotter.

Harness racing is the other major form of horse racing, but in it the horses are of course restricted to the two-time gaits. As it is natural for the horse to gallop when trying to go as fast as possible, rather than trot or pace, the natural horse has had to be changed a good deal through breeding and training for this form of horse racing.

The trot and pace are used in harness racing because they are both much smoother gaits for the pulling of carriages as the horse stays on the horizontal and does not tip up and down, as in the canter or gallop. Trotting and pacing are thus essential for modern harness racing in which the carriages are very light, and was also the favoured pace for harness work particularly during the eighteenth and nineteenth centuries, when a popular form of speedy transportation in Britain was a light carriage pulled by the Norfolk Trotter. This highly prized and useful breed was the result of crossing local trotting mares (horses renowned for their trotting are mentioned in Britain as early as the fifteenth century) with selected descendants of the Darley Arabian, one of the founders of the thoroughbred breed.

Following the growth of flat racing most European countries and America tried another form – namely harness racing. The Norfolk Trotter was the most renowned breed for this work and during the early nineteenth century it was exported to America, the Nether-

lands, France and other countries in Europe where it acted as foundation stock for their new sport.

The aim in all these countries was to speed up the trot, so the thoroughbred was used extensively in this initial cross-breeding. Other breeds used were hackneys (Britain's descendants of the Norfolk Trotter), Arabs, Barbs and local breeds such as the Morgan in the United States, Anglo-Norman in France and Mecklenburg in Russia.

Today the American Standardbred is generally recognized as the world's fastest trotter. The foundation sire for the breed was the thoroughbred Messenger, exported from Britain in 1790, and the Norfolk Trotter Bellfounder. The breed was developed in the nineteenth century, first by judicious cross-breeding until no further excellence could be added, and thereafter by line-breeding.

As with the thoroughbred, the criterion of excellence for breeding Standardbreds was performance on the racetrack. As its name implies, standards were set for this sport: trotters had to cover a mile (1.6km) in 2 minutes 30 seconds, pacers the same distance in 5 seconds less.

During the nineteenth century the sport and breeds for harness racing developed rapidly in Europe and America. Russia, however, had been ahead of them. In 1775 Count Orlov crossed his Arab stallion Smetanka with an imported Danish mare, and the offspring was the start of the Orlov Trotter. Further cross-breeding was carried out with Dutch mares, Arabs and the extensively used English thoroughbred and Norfolk Trotter. The Orlov Trotter remained world famous throughout the nineteenth century, but by the twentieth century the Americans' selective breeding policy had paid off and the Orlov's times and performance had been surpassed by Standardbreds. The Russians, eager for the best, imported some of the American breed and the result was the faster Metis Trotter.

COMPETITION HORSES

Breeds: Thoroughbred type and warmbloods – Hanoverian, Trakehner, Holstein, Swedish, Dutch and Danish Warmbloods, Selle Français (*Note:* most European nations now have a national breed or, in the case of Germany, regional breeds of competition horses.)

The most fundamental changes brought about in horses this century have been with regard to competition horses. It is the Olympic equestrian sports – show jumping, dressage and horse trials – which have boomed in the twentieth century, and likewise the production of horses for them.

It has not been easy to develop a horse with the attributes needed for competitions. No country has yet produced a

A warmblood stallion showing great athleticism and strength, two vital assets in a competition horse. This is the Danish Warmblood Atlantis. Like many other breeds of warmbloods he has Hanoverians among his ancestors.

The Ardennes, one of the coldbloods, heavy breeds used extensively in the past for agriculture, transport and industry. Today few are used for work but some have been cross-bred with more refined breeds to produce warmbloods.

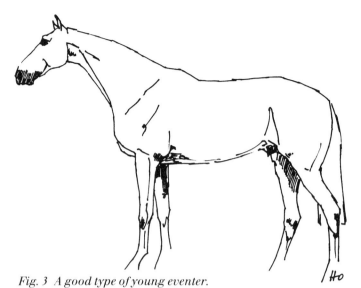

Fig. 3 A good type of young eventer.

breed which cannot be bettered, as was the case with the thoroughbred. The talents needed for success in competitions are more numerous than in racing, and less easily measured than is speed. The most famous competition breed, the Hanoverian, has its goal defined as 'a correctly built, noble, versatile warmblood horse, capable of superior performance under saddle, with big ground covering, yet light and elastic gaits, good temperament and honest character' – all of which is rather more vague than the ability to be fast enough to win races.

Another factor contributing to the many different competition breeds is that competitive success is based on a partnership. In competitions horse and rider have to suit one another (in racing, on the other hand, this is of little account: most horses will only run better for another jockey if he is more able, not because they get on with him better); consequently each country tends to favour a type of horse which suits its national attitudes. Thus the German horses are powerful, strong, and work best if well disciplined. French horses are more flamboyant and highly spirited, benefiting from riders who are fast-thinking and give them a greater variety of activities. English horses are noted for their boldness; they never give up but respond better to a mental rather than a physical partnership, based on cooperation rather than discipline. The tendency therefore has been for each nation to develop its own breed of competition horse.

The English-speaking nations have not yet gone this far, but have relied on the horses which already existed, their thoroughbred types. These were either thoroughbreds which had never got to or had retired from racing, or hunters which were traditionally by thoroughbreds and out of any one of a great variety of mares, rarely pedigree, but boasting the features often lacking in the thoroughbred, namely substance, common sense and strength.

These are the horses which have been used for hunting for two hundred or more years. They are not a breed, for the sires are thoroughbreds; half-bred colts are gelded, so there is constant cross-breeding in the production of hunters.

These thoroughbred types have excelled in the closest sport to hunting, horse trials, in which the thoroughbred's speed, courage and 'class' are great attributes, but the jumps are not so high nor the dressage test so difficult for greater athletic ability to be demanded.

The thoroughbred type, either pure bred or with a dash of common blood, has helped the Americans, British and Irish to win many medals in horse trials. This same type has had some success in show jumping and dressage also, but with speed, 'class' and courage not being so vital, and with the rise in standard of these sports, the European warmbloods, selectively bred for competitions, now dominate the prizes.

Although the British have a claim to being the best selective breeders through the successful development of the thoroughbred they, unlike all the other Europeans, have not used these methods for competition horses. Since the Second World War Belgians, Austrians, Danes, Dutch, Swiss and Irish have all developed their own particular brand of competition horse, and the Germans, Swedes and French started their breeding policy much earlier. This policy has been to change, through selective breeding, their

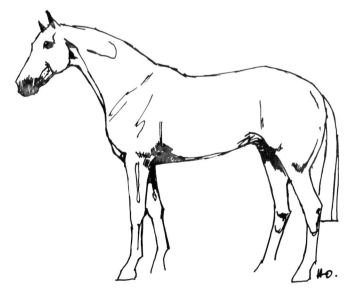

Fig. 4 A good type of young show jumper.

cavalry and carriage horses into the more refined and athletic horses in demand today. It is indicative of the soundness of this strategy that the nations which have followed it the longest and most thoroughly – Germany, Sweden and France – have by far the best records at the equestrian Olympic Games.

The record holders in this group are, perhaps surprisingly, the Swedes. The Swedish cavalry won so many Olympic gold medals before its disbandment in the 1950s that they still have more than any other country in the world. A brief study of how their horses were changed from remounts into competitors is illuminating and also typical of what happened in the rest of Europe as the demand for competition horses escalated.

The Swedes had imported horses for cross-breeding during the nineteenth century but it was only in the last quarter of the century that they began serious selective breeding. Their breeding goals were stamina, endurance, good temperament and athletic ability. With time the emphasis switched more to the latter, for the remounts came to be used less as vital instruments of war and more as competition horses.

A government stud book was started in 1874, with entry confined to breeding stock which had been examined and found to be sound and suitable. This set a standard and provided pedigrees to help in further selection.

The stallions had to attain higher standards than the mares. Apart from having to possess the visual attributes of soundness, conformation and action, and the hereditary ones of a good pedigree, the Swedish riding horses were put through performance testing, just like racehorses. The horse was tested in the type of activity for which it was breeding progeny (dressage, show jumping or cross-country) and records were kept of reactions during training and tests, to help evaluate character. The tests both ensured a high standard of stallions for breeding, and also helped the breeder to find in which sphere a stallion excelled or was disappointing so that a complementary selection between mare and stallion could be made.

Stallions could not breed unless they passed these tests, and they did not receive a full licence until the progeny had been examined. Any sign of hereditary defects in young stock meant the end of a stallion's career at stud. Thus standards were high and information to help breeders was freely available. An additional aid to the success of this policy was government involvement which financed national studs at Flyinge and Strömsholm (the latter was closed when the cavalry was disbanded).

Initially the Swedes practised a large amount of cross-

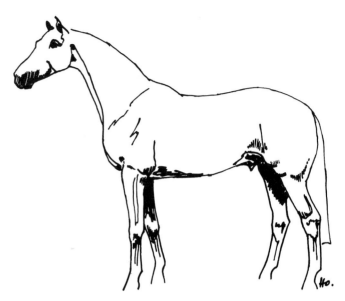

Fig. 5 A good type of young dressage horse.

breeding. Native Swedish mares were mainly used, but stallions were imported, particularly thoroughbreds, Hanoverians and Trakehners. As the Swedish Warmblood began to establish itself as a top competition horse the cross-breeding was reduced, and line-breeding and outcrossing used more and more. The Swedes have not closed their stud book, however; if the Swedish authorities feel that their breed is showing signs of lacking a required feature they quickly import a stallion with these features. This use of other breeds to reinforce features that are disappearing or never existed distinguishes the Swedish and all other European warmbloods from the thoroughbred and other pure breeds. The qualities needed in competition horses are still changing, for the format of competitions has not yet stabilized, and because the zenith in quality of competition horses has not been reached, breeders are willing to adapt and change. The purity of the breed is secondary to providing the best possible competition horse.

Thus the Swedish Warmblood was developed by changing the tough little remounts through injections of mainly Hanoverian, Trakehner and thoroughbred blood. But this was done only selectively. The Swedes were among the first to apply calculated cross-breeding, rigorous testing, careful compilation of records and use of scientific principles to the breeding of competition horses, and they reaped the benefits by winning so many gold medals.

Their major rivals were the Germans, and the Swedes made use of them by importing Hanoverian and Trakehner blood. The Hanoverian must be mentioned here, for not

A good type of brood mare showing off her gaits with her foal. She is a Hanoverian, the most successful breed of warmbloods in the world. The substance and athleticism seen here in both mare and foal show clearly the reasons for this success.

A hunter displaying its most valued asset – the gallop. Hunters are types not breeds, as they do not breed true to type but are the result of cross-breeding, usually between the thoroughbred and a non-pedigree, heavier type of mare.

only is it the most famous competition horse today, not only is it a foundation breed for the younger warmbloods of other countries, but it has a much longer history than the Swedish Warmblood and one full of changes. The breed allegedly began in the form of great war horses back in the sixteenth century, and these were certainly being refined into renowned carriage horses with military value in the eighteenth and nineteenth centuries. In the twentieth century the demand for carriage horses fell dramatically, but cavalry, artillery and agricultural horses were all needed so the Hanoverian was suitably changed to provide these types. More recently competitions have become important and the other uses have declined, so it has been converted into a fine riding horse.

The Hanoverian has thus been progressively refined over the centuries by injections of thoroughbred, Arab and Trakehner blood, but in restricted proportions. The Hanoverian Society had a better and numerically larger base to work from than the Swedes, so their competition horse was developed with far less cross-breeding. Today thoroughbreds may only make up 10 per cent of the stallions at the state stud of Celle, and all of them must have a good record on the racetrack before joining these elite stables. Three per cent are Trakehners and just one per cent Arabs. Other countries, apart from France, tend to use greater percentages of outside blood in their warmbloods.

The Hanoverian breed was given official status by George II who founded the Celle stud in 1735, and from this date matings were recorded and identification certificates issued. Stallions had to pass conformation tests as long ago as 1844 but it was not until 1928 that the training and testing of young stallions was begun. Today these tests are some of the most rigorous in Europe. The state stallions have to undergo eleven months of training and observation beforehand and are subjected to other veterinary, conformation, pedigree, performance and progeny tests. The result is that only 2 per cent of the Hanoverian colts born are allowed to stand as stallions. This strict selection is possible because the Hanoverian is one of the most numerous warmbloods, boasting of nearly 17,000 mares good enough to have passed the strict tests needed for registration in the stud book. This enables higher standards to be enforced than in countries where the number of warmbloods is limited, and facilitates the making of changes within the breed rather than by cross-breeding.

The intelligent, athletic Swedish Warmblood and the powerful mover and jumper the Hanoverian have, through the far-sighted and strict policies of their societies, become the leading breeds of competition horses. Their success,

however, has spurred others in the attempt to produce the competition horse for which there is such a heavy demand. The Westphalians, also from Germany, are becoming very fashionable. These are neighbours and close relations of the Hanoverian, and rose to prominence with such great horses as Ahlerich (1982 World Dressage Champion) and Fire (1982 World Show Jumping Champion). The Selle Français, athletic and spirited, are based mainly on the Anglo-Norman, Anglo-Arab and some trotter stock. They are gaining prestige with such high-class international representatives as the great jumping stallion Galoubet. The compact and springy Dutch Warmblood's foundations date from after the Second World War and the blood used has in the main been that of the native carriage horses, Gelderland and Gröningen, plus some thoroughbred (mainly French) and Hanoverian. Dutch Warmbloods have many stars, and the most valuable, Calypso, jumps for the United States.

The newest successful breed is the Danish Warmblood which has an exceptionally trainable temperament. The Danes only started selective breeding for competitions in the 1960s and had to import heavily to cross-breed Hanoverian, Swedish, Trakehner, thoroughbred and Oldenburg, but they can already boast of gold medals in the European Championships and substitute Olympics of 1980.

Some people might wonder why, in this account of breeding horses for dressage, no mention has been made of the Lipizzaners who entrance spectators at the most famous dressage school in the world, the Spanish Riding School in Vienna, nor of the Andalusians who perform magnificently in the Spanish and Portuguese schools in particular. These indeed are the breeds that had been doing dressage long before the cavalry took it up. The distinction is that these horses were bred for *haute école* – to achieve great collection, to perform airs above the ground and other highly gymnastic movements. Few, however, are capable of lengthening their strides into the extended trots and canters which are a vital part of dressage tests. The cavalry wanted horses which could accelerate rapidly for galloping into battle, and the dressage tests were devised to test this 'sporting' aspect rather than the artistic one of dramatic movement. The competitive dressage horse is more of a gymnast than a dancer, closer to a show jumper than those eye-catching, high-stepping Lipizzaners and Andalusians. The warmbloods answer the requirements of competitive dressage much better than these traditional breeds of dressage horse.

All over Europe the formula for breeding competition horses is refining the army, agricultural and native stock of the various countries with thoroughbred and some Arab blood, improved with already successful competition blood such as the Hanoverian, Trakehner, Swedish and Selle Français, in order to produce national breeds at top competition level. Each breed so far has distinctive features despite the international cross-breeding. It will be interesting to see whether these are maintained, or whether with the continuing development of competitions there will be such internationalization that differences in national styles, methods and approaches are reduced to one 'best' way, and the horses in consequence become one 'best' breed like the thoroughbred.

COMBINED DRIVING

Breeds: Hungarian, Gelderland, Holstein, Hanoverian, Cleveland Bay, Welsh Cob, Kladruber

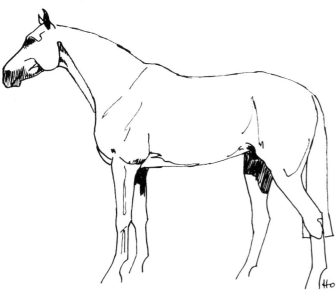

Fig. 6 A good type of young driving horse.

This three-day event on wheels only started as an international sport in 1960. Competitors have been able to utilize the breeds which had been developed commercially for carriage driving during the eighteenth and nineteenth centuries, and in this century for fun. These carriage horses are big, powerful breeds, capable of drawing heavy coaches for miles along rough roads and tracks.

Many of the fast growing numbers of competitors in combined driving have found these horses rather large for manoeuvring around the tricky obstacles in the cross-country section. Consequently there has recently been some cross-breeding to refine these breeds, using the small thoroughbred with the Cleveland Bay, Holstein, Kladruber, Lipizzaner and Hanoverian. Another popular breed is the

Welsh Cob, which was not bred as a coach horse but as an all-round riding, harness and even racing (trotting) performer for Welsh farmers. It is smaller and more athletic than the traditional carriage horses but has proved a little gassy and high spirited as a combined driving horse – for which, as will be seen in the training section, a vital factor is an unflappable temperament. More docile breeds have therefore been used for cross-breeding with the Welsh Cob.

The most popular breed of horse for combined driving is the Hungarian. This has been bred for centuries in the country in which coaching allegedly started in the sixteenth century, in the town of Kocs from which the word 'coach' was derived. The Hungarian horse is smaller, more energetic and athletic than the other European coaching breeds, and so is better suited to combined driving.

Combined driving has little more than a decade of history, and this is not long enough to establish what improvements can be made through breeding. Time will tell whether the indications of the trends in breeding outlined here will produce a horse with the necessary strength, stamina and manoeuvrability for this young sport.

POLO

Breeds: Argentinian, thoroughbred

The rigorous selective methods of breeding which have changed rather ordinary breeds into highly talented racehorses, trotters, show jumpers and dressage horses have not been applied in polo.

Luck and nature have produced a wonderful foundation for the polo pony, the Criollo. These ponies developed their

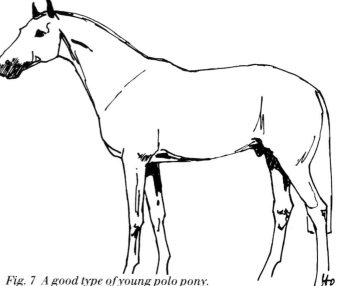

Fig. 7 A good type of young polo pony.

The champion Arab stallion Bravado. The Arab and the thoroughbred are known as hotbloods. These hotbloods are (and have been for hundreds of years) used to refine and add class to other types of horses.

The Cleveland Bay, one of the older breeds of warmbloods. The Cleveland's major use was as a carriage horse or all-rounder for the farmer, but it has been maintained as a pure-bred and not refined like the European warmbloods in order to meet the modern demand for competition horses.

special features – toughness, powers of acceleration and manoeuvrability – through having to survive wild on the vast plains of the Pampas in Argentina. Allegedly the basic stock was a shipload of Andalusians and light draught animals that landed in Buenos Aires in 1535 but were soon set free when the Indians sacked the city. Adaptation to the rough conditions over hundreds of years resulted in the Criollos, which were eventually caught and used as cow ponies on the *haciendas*. With the advent of polo they were put to the speedier thoroughbreds, and the result was the most popular polo pony in the world.

Most of the polo playing nations have imported large numbers of Argentinian polo ponies including enough mares to start breeding their own stock.

The alternative to the Argentinian pony is the small thoroughbred (polo ponies must be under 15.3 hh). These are particularly successful where the thoroughbreds are tougher and have led a less pampered life than the expensive specimens found in the United States, Britain and France. Thus New Zealand, in particular, has produced good thoroughbred polo ponies, as there the thoroughbreds spend more time out at grass, less in the stables being filled with oats, and the result is a tougher animal which can better withstand the galloping, turning and barging on the polo field.

THE WESTERN HORSE

Breeds: Quarter Horse, Appaloosa, Pinto and Paint

Western riding covers a wide range of activities based on ranch and trail work of cowboys in days gone by. The

Fig. 8 A good type of western horse.

horses originally used for these purposes were utility stock, often randomly bred and raised in free-roaming herds. These 'cow ponies' were generally small (14 hh or less) and coarse, but they were tough, thrifty and agile and therefore well suited to the harsh environment in which they worked.

Many of the horses used today in western competitions are descended from cow ponies, but the standard of these competitions, like all equestrian sports, is constantly improving. Specialized talents are demanded and these all-round tough 'cow ponies' have been refined and upgraded to reach the higher requirements through outcrosses, mostly with thoroughbreds and Arabs.

The modern offspring of the old cow ponies usually qualify for one of the four of the American breed registers – the Quarter Horse, Appaloosa, Pinto or Paint. The multicoloured Appaloosas, Pintos and Paints were traditionally the horses of the Indians. The original stock was said to be mainly Spanish or Portuguese, brought to the New World during the seventeenth century. The Indians valued and nurtured these horses, for they found them tough and their multi-colours were good camouflage.

The other main source of western horses is the Quarter Horse. This compact powerful breed is also thought to have developed from Spanish stock (mainly Andalusian and Barb), brought to America in the seventeenth century. It was crossed with the thoroughbred, for the early test of this breed, and its purpose, was to race over quarter mile stretches – hence its name. Today Quarter Horses are mainly used as racehorses over sprint distances. They are the most numerous breed in the United States, and their powers of quick acceleration, strength, agility and good temperament make them excellent horses for western riding.

In the twentieth century equestrian sports have become big business. As in other types of sport, the days of the amateur all-rounder reaching the top are gone. Not only must humans and equines be born with particular natural talents, they must also undergo specialized, time-consuming training. Careful selective breeding can, as we have seen, be used to increase a horse's natural talents for a particular activity. In racing, one of the oldest sports considered, the horse has already been developed into 'the' best type. The process of establishing the best breed for the other sports is in varying stages according to the length of their existence, their popularity and the commercial returns for the participants. The harness racers are nearest to this goal, dressage, eventers and show jumpers are on the way, but the 'baby', international combined driving, is only just beginning.

CHANGES THROUGH TRAINING

Dressage

David Hunt

INTRODUCTION

Dressage is simply the training of the horse to make it more athletic and gymnastic, to help it develop its natural ability so that it can do its work with greater ease, balance and elegance. At its basic levels all the various types of horses considered in this book practise dressage, for it helps them to jump higher, turn quicker and even gallop faster. At more advanced levels, however, dressage entails teaching the horse difficult gymnastic exercises so that it becomes an end in itself and ultimately an art. The very best dressage riders are artists capable of using their horse as a means of expression.

All the movements required of a dressage horse are based on those he performs naturally when free. An athletic young horse running wild is often seen spinning around (the basis of the pirouette), reversing (rein back), moving sideways (shoulder-in and half pass), changing legs in the canter (flying change), in a highly elevated trot (passage) and trotting on the spot (piaffe). The major differences between the actions a horse might perform in freedom and those under the rider are that the horse has to adjust its balance to carry the weight of the rider; correct training will also give it greater suppleness, power and control.

This control comes from developing collection, which is the central aim of dressage training. Collection is worked for progressively from the very early stages. It entails the shortening and heightening of the steps whilst maintaining the fluency of the natural gait. This shortening and

Fig. 9 These illustrations show how through careful training the horse's point of balance is gradually transferred towards the hindquarters. As a novice the horse is on its forehand (left) but as it learns to carry greater weight with its hindquarters it becomes correspondingly more manoeuvrable, lighter and more powerful.

heightening is achieved by compressing and rounding the horse's frame (Fig. 9). The centre of balance of its natural elongated outline is gradually moved backwards by lowering its hindquarters, placing the hindlegs further underneath its body and raising its forehand. The weight is increasingly transferred from the forehand to the hindquarters. Thus a young horse might take twenty steps to cover 20 metres, but as collection is acquired the same distance can be covered in thirty, then forty steps.

With collection the horse has greater power to extend or even to jump and gallop; it has greater manoeuvrability and is easier to control, for with more weight carried by the hindlegs its forehand is lighter and freer to move. Collection makes the horse a more pleasant ride and a more exciting one, capable of a far greater range of movement then in the natural untrained state.

Dressage horses are used for many purposes – some simply to give their riders daily pleasure in work at home, others to give magnificent artistic displays like those of the Spanish Riding School in Vienna. The majority, however, are aimed at competitions. These take the form of tests in which a specific series of movements are awarded marks from 1 to 10. The tests range from very easy, in which no more than simple walk, trot and canter are required, to the Grand Prix Special which determines Olympic and World Champions. In this, the ultimate test, the horse must prove that it has been very well trained, showing that the natural ability has been enhanced so that the paces have more spring, are more free, elastic and soft, that its body has been developed so that it has great control and is able to use this to perform very difficult movements, and that it obeys willingly but not subserviently.

NATURAL TALENTS

Most horses can be trained to do most of the dressage movements in a fashion; but to do them with the quality and ease that gives pleasure to riders and onlookers and gains high marks from the judges, the horse needs to be born with the shape, movement and character particularly suited to this work.

The shape

A naturally high head carriage will help in the advanced work, but a head and neck set lower are a great help in the novice stages where a more horizontal outline is required. It is, however, better that the horse should be going against his natural bearing at this easier stage, rather than in the

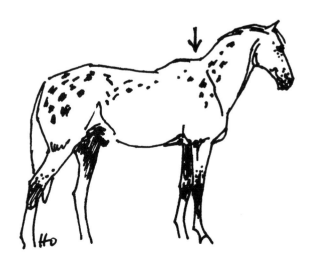

Fig. 10 A poor shape for dressage as the horse lacks a harmonious curve from the wither into the neck.

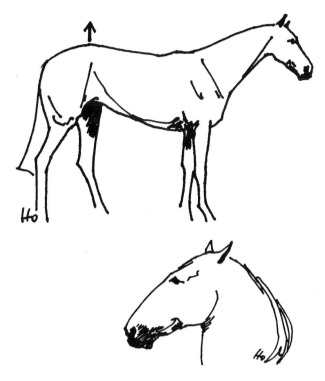

Fig. 11 Further deficiencies. The horse (top) is croup high – the hindquarters are higher than the forehand which will make it difficult for the horse to transfer its weight off the forehand. The small eye of the horse below is often a sign of a mean character.

difficult Grand Prix work which, for collection, demands the lowering of the hindquarters and the raising of the forehand and therefore a high head carriage. The head and neck must be well set on to a good wither, for any breaks at this vital point (Fig. 10) mean a break in the muscles connecting the hindquarters and the head, and a consequent loss of the vital coordination of all the limbs.

Again, with the ultimate aim of high collection and the necessity to drop the hindquarters, it will make the work difficult if the latter are higher than the forehand (croup high). In this case it would be natural for the horse to push the weight on to its shoulder and the forehand rather than to carry it with the hindquarters. Ideally the head, shoulder and croup should be on a downward slope with the head the highest point (as in collection).

The overall shape is best when not too compact, for the short-backed horse will find it more difficult to become supple. A neat, 'perfect' conformation sought after for showing classes (equine beauty contests) is all too often a bit stuffy. For dressage, it is the athlete that is needed, not the pretty, fancy types; the beauty is in the movement, not the shape when standing still.

Temperament

Flashy, eye-catching horses are (like pretty women) all too often a disappointment as one gets to know them. They tend to lack substance in their character, and the ability to enjoy work. Much more important is that the horse should be proud, catching one's attention because it is alert and notices everything. It is this indefinable quality of 'presence' which earns the extra marks in tests; then performances are never dull and riding is more fun because the horse is interested in its surroundings.

A dressage horse has to be obedient but must do the work because it wants to, not because it is sober and too easy-going to rebel. An easy-going person is rarely a real friend, because the ups and downs and confrontations are needed to establish the give and take of deep friendship. Similarly the sober horse never gives, but just does as required when ridden hard. A good dressage horse may be naughty at times and have disagreements with its rider, but it will also help him and try to do the work required.

The horse cannot be such a rebel as to lose its temper. It has to accept control by the rider and, although the vital strength of character will be lacking if it never puts up a struggle, the training will be tiring and unproductive if it fights every day.

Fig. 12 This horse has an excellent bold eye, and its alert expression draws one towards looking at it. This is the valuable asset known as 'presence'.

Training the horse at the canter. The animal is showing a good lift to the stride, with the forehand coming well off the ground and the hindquarters taking a fair proportion of the weight. Although David Hunt is not wearing a hat, equestrian societies recommend that riders should always do so, even during training.

David Hunt lunging a horse which is showing a good working trot. The lunge-rein is taut, and this is important – the pressure should be consistent, thus helping the horse to remain in balance and to describe a true circle.

The shape of the eye and the way it moves are good indications of whether a horse has a suitable temperament for dressage. Round, bold eyes set well apart are promising. Small, mean, nervously flashing eyes are warning signs.

If the horse can be ridden, it may be put under pressure and the reactions considered. If it naturally wants to go at for example 7 mph (11 kph), then it may be compressed and made to go at 5 mph (8 kph). The manner in which it accepts or rebels against this control is a useful indication of character.

Action

Movement is the crucial factor in a dressage horse. If the horse moves well, almost any other problem can be overcome, for with correct athletic movement, the work will be easy and natural.

The joints in all the limbs – hock, knee, fetlock, stifle and elbow – must bend easily in all gaits. Of particular importance is the hock joint; if there is natural flexion to this, particularly in the canter, the piaffe and passage should be relatively easy to establish.

At the walk the horse should use its whole body, so that when the front foot is lowered towards the ground it takes the whole body with it. The strides should be long and sweeping so that the hind feet are placed beyond the footprint of the corresponding foreleg (known as over tracking). There is danger, however, in the exceptional walker which takes ponderous long strides, as although these earn the highest marks, the horse is often a slow

thinker. A slightly more controlled, less extravagant walker is a safer bet.

When trotting, the natural length of strides should be closer to collection than extension, for it is easier to train a horse to lengthen its paces than to elevate into collection. The action should be rounded, fluent and supple, with the knee and hock joints being used fairly equally so that the action of the hind legs and forelegs is harmonious. The forefeet should point to the place where they will land, and follow the path of an arc so that the feet come down flat. Rounded strides are more desirable than showy, angular, sweeping strides, for the latter action tends to be less supple and controllable and more earthbound. It must be natural for a dressage horse to spring off the ground in both trot and canter, to be light on its feet and to be happy to spend time in the air; in this way it will be easier for it to shorten the body, elevate the strides and collect.

At the canter the joints should bend rather like a piston and the horse should show the potential to be able to canter on the spot, for then pirouettes will be easy. The action at the canter should be rounded, with a natural lift that with each stride brings the forehand further off the ground than the hindquarters, thus making collection easier.

CHANGES THROUGH TRAINING
Character

The dressage horse must accept discipline without having its character destroyed. A 'spooky' horse, one that is lively and reacts to its surroundings, can, for example, be an asset

Fig. 13 A horse which has been trained to develop the correct muscles, along the top line in particular.

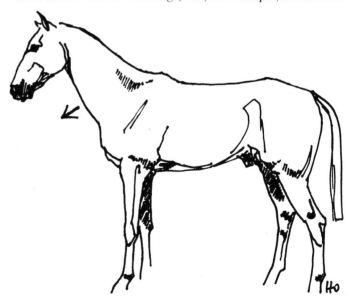

Fig. 14 A horse which has failed to develop the correct muscles and instead has incorrect muscles on the underside of its neck.

as long as this tendency is directed in a forward manner and so used to enhance presence. Thus if it spooks it should not be punished, but attempts should be made to turn its attention elsewhere. A keenness to observe is what gives a horse presence, and it is this which gives it the edge over more ordinary horses in a dressage test. The presence must not be drilled out of a horse, but rather controlled and directed in a constructive manner to prevent it being used as an excuse not to work.

The dressage horse needs to be disciplined – but not harangued – in every sphere of its life. Consistent reward and reprimand for what is right and wrong should be applied at all times, in the stable and even when hacking out.

Conformation

Good dressage training will change the horse by making it better looking, just as body-building lessons give a man a better figure. The muscles which should be developed are those along its top line (Fig. 13). The neck must become more crested, the back more rounded, for both the shape and the steps of the dressage horse should be arched and rounded.

This roundness will only be achieved if the horse is worked correctly; if it is not, the wrong muscles, such as those on the underside of the neck, will develop. Muscular development is indicative of the way a horse has been worked.

Movement

The natural movement of the horse must be maintained and improved through training. The first vital consideration is the regularity and sequence of the paces. The

Fig. 15 A horse showing good freedom at the walk. It is overtracking, the hind hoofprint coming further forward than the fore hoofprint on the same side.

natural sequence to the paces can be lost through tension, resistance or similar problems. The most easily lost is the four-time marching pace of the walk: the intervals between the hoofbeats become unequal and sometimes only two hoofbeats are heard (known as pacing). To avoid such problems the work at the walk must be kept very relaxed.

The trot should always be two-time, the legs moving in diagonal pairs with a moment of suspension in between.

The canter is a three-beat pace, followed like the trot by a moment of suspension. It is, however, all too easy with incorrect work (for example trying to collect by slowing down rather than elevating and shortening the strides) for the pair of diagonals to separate and for four hoof beats to be heard.

The first aim therefore with regard to the paces is to preserve their natural sequence. All dressage work is

Fig. 16 Various types of trot. The horse on the left shows a pleasing round outline and good flexion of the joints. Although the centre horse is taking long strides they are rather flat and there will be little suspension, while the horse on the right is flicking its forelegs and this produces stiffness.

The half pass, when the horse goes forwards and sideways simultaneously. David Hunt is in a pleasing balance with his horse which has established a good bend.

Left: Training the horse for piaffe. Here David Hunt has established some good steps for this, the most difficult movement in dressage.

Fig. 17 A good natural canter with the horse showing a rounded stride and a pronounced moment of suspension.

Fig. 18 A flat canter with the weight falling on to the forehand. This limits power and manoeuvrability, and the aim of training is to get the horse to carry more weight with its hindquarters.

Fig. 19 This horse gives the feeling of cantering uphill, with the forehand high and the hindquarters taking a good proportion of the weight.

aimed at maintaining and enhancing the horse's natural movement.

The movements should be fluid but firm, rather like the flow of oil from a jug which has a bit of 'hand' or elasticity to it. A tiger in slow motion displays the aimed-for action – a great sense of power with loose and supple movement.

In the trot the activity of the strides should be matched by their elevation. The joints should flex well (activity) and there should be a discernible moment when all the feet are off the ground. If the strides are flat and earthbound it will be difficult to achieve collection. If the knee and hock bend well yet there is little elevation the horse is not taking the movement up and through the body (see page 40). If on the other hand there is great elevation without activity the horse will lose its suppleness and begin to stiffen in this unnatural trot.

At the canter the strides should gain cadence and lightness, becoming rounded with a definite moment of suspension and a pronounced rhythm. The flat canter of the untrained horse when the weight falls on to the forehand and the speed often varies may be changed through careful training into a controlled, balanced, rhythmical and powerful pace.

The other vital change to the gaits brought about by training enables the length of the strides to vary from the shortest (collected) to working, to medium, to the longest (extended), as in Fig. 20. The untrained horse starts at the working gaits, the length of stride most natural to him. Once the balance, regularity and suppleness of steps is established, the rider can progressively ask the horse to change the length of its strides, to shorten and lengthen, but without losing any of the vital assets of the gaits established at working trot and canter. This training makes a dressage horse as fit as a racehorse, although in a different way. The racehorse is the runner, the dressage horse the gymnast. Thus the latter should have tremendous muscle tone and great power in reserve even at the end of the test, but his lungs and heart will not have been extended like those of the racehorse.

Developing muscle tone is a very slow process. Horses need a certain amount of rest, but turning them out in a field for a few weeks means that they lose tone and have to go through the dreary (and sometimes painful) process of rebuilding the muscles. Thus dressage horses are best given two or three short breaks a year, lasting two to three weeks each, when they are turned out by day but kept in at night and well fed. In this way they are freshened up without losing too much muscle. In other equestrian sports where endurance is tested, such as racing and eventing,

longer breaks are needed to restore mental vigour, and as muscle tone is less important these are not a handicap.

TRAINING

The changes made to the dressage horse through training are achieved largely by adhering to certain very important principles.

The first of these is rhythm. This is easiest to establish with a horse which is built off its forehand, that is with strong hindquarters which are lower than the forehand and therefore more able to carry the weight. With this conformation it is much easier for the horse to find a balance and therefore a rhythm, for rhythm is easy to establish in a balanced horse. Some breeds, the European warmblood breeds in particular, have a natural rhythm, which makes training easier.

The rider must always be conscious of the rhythm; it must be so much part of his system that as soon as he mounts a horse he sets about maintaining or achieving it. He should have a metronome in his mind. His aim is to establish such a rhythm in the horse that the reins can be slackened without it affecting the pace at all. This rhythm should be maintained throughout all the work, so the rider must not ask so much (too small a circle, too tight a corner) that the horse loses its balance and therefore the rhythm.

Many riders find it easier to establish a rhythm when sitting to the trot. Thus at the beginning of each schooling session the first few strides of trot may be sitting, but as

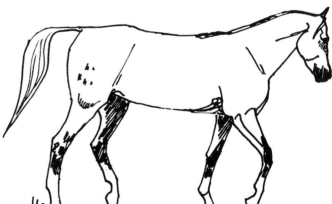

Fig. 20 Training enables the horse to vary the length of its stride. This horse is trotting (top) when collected, (centre) with medium strides and (below) with the longest strides possible – the extended trot.

Fig. 21 A horse which is 'built on its forehand'. It will be difficult for such a horse to transfer its balance to the hindquarters and establish rhythm to its work.

This is the dressage arena, around which five judges are positioned. In this area of 60 × 20 metres competitors are alone for between eight and eleven minutes (according to the type of test) and have to perform at their best possible level.

To enable a horse to make the most of its ability the rider must remain in balance with the horse and must not slip even a fraction to one side or forwards or backwards when turning corners or performing movements. Such unity of balance is here beautifully achieved by leading international rider Anne-Marie Sanders Keyzer on Amon.

soon as the rhythm is found rising trot is best, as this allows the muscles in the horse's back to loosen up and work before sitting.

'Swinging through'

It is vital that the horse should swing through its back when working. This means that the power goes through the body, and that the muscles from the hindquarters to the jaw work freely, so that all the actions of the horse are coordinated and connected. No group of muscles should resist, tense up and so block the movement through the body. This happens most usually in the muscles of the back or the neck in front of the wither. A horse which thus swings is using all of its body and not just sections of it. The rider is not sitting on a board, beneath which the horse's legs move independently back and forth.

Athletic, supple horses naturally work through the back. Any horse that does so will have elasticity in its steps. There will be an upsurge and downsurge, with lift coming through the body and more suspension in the trot and canter. The strides appear to be almost in slow motion in comparison to the stiff horse which simply swings its legs.

It is this working through the back which gives the movement softness, suppleness and an eye-catching quality. It makes the horse a more comfortable ride and a more exhilarating one, for the rider has greater control over the entire body of the horse.

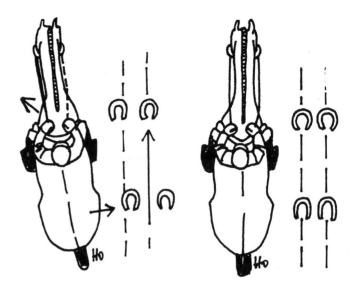

Fig. 23 Straightness is an important attribute. In the diagram on the left the horse's hind legs are not following in the same tracks as the corresponding forelegs. This makes it difficult to contain energy and give the horse power.

Straightness

The horse must work through equally on both sides of its body. Each hock should work as much as the other and its action go up through the body, neck and head to the horse's jaw, where it is felt through the reins by the rider's hands. If the horse is straight there should be an equal feel in both reins, but such straightness is not inborn. Horses, like humans, are naturally one-sided, and a great deal of time during training is spent in softening up the stiff side, straightening up the naturally curved side.

As already pointed out, the central aim of dressage is the progressive compression of the horse's body into greater and greater collection. Gradually, over the years, the horse is mentally and physically trained to accept this compression, enabling it to contain energy, rather like a spring. This is known as impulsion. If the horse is not straight, much of the driving force put into its body by activating the hind legs will disappear out to the side (like a bent spring). Only when the horse is straight, with the muscle tone equalized on both sides, can the energy created by the active hind legs be contained by the restraining action of the rider's hands (likewise, if you push one end of a spring to compress it you must also restrain the other end).

Softness in the jaw

Straightness can be seen if there is no kink in the body – although there will be slight flexion to the inside of a circle,

Fig. 22 A horse which is stiff in the back and neck. The hind legs are being dragged and it is not 'swinging through' like the horse in Fig. 25.

pirouette and half pass – and it will be felt in the equal contact in both reins. This pressure through the reins should be soft and elastic, for softness in the jaw is another principle to be worked for during training. The horse must learn to accept and want to stay with the rider's hand, for if it tries to fight against the pressure its back will be braced. The rider should try to soften his feel through the reins,

Fig. 24 This horse is remaining 'on the bit' at the collected walk.

Fig. 25 This horse has a well set on neck and head which helps it to come 'on the bit'. It is also showing the ability to work through with a supple swinging back.

asking the horse to relax its jaw, and first to 'accept the bit', then come 'on the bit'. In the former the horse accepts contact with the rider through the reins, but through progressive training learns to work 'through' the back, to be straight, and to be soft in the jaw which enables it to establish an outline from which it is easy to perform. Then the horse is said to be 'on the bit'. In this position the poll is the highest point of the neck, which is more or less arched and raised according to the degree of collection; the head is steady and on or just in front of the vertical; and the hocks are being used actively under the hindquarters.

Some horses are described as being born 'on the bit'; they will not be fighting against nature to achieve this vital aspect of dressage. Such a horse will have its head and neck set on correctly, enabling the muscles to operate freely, and therefore it can easily work through to establish an elastic, soft contact with the rider through the reins. Stiffness in the muscles (the blocks) usually arise at the points where the wither joins the neck, and the head the neck (at the poll and jowel). If these joining points are angular or restricted or broken, rather than curved and smooth, the muscles tend to become blocked and the horse will then resist.

TIME SCHEDULE

It takes an experienced rider four to five years to train a good horse to Grand Prix standard. The talented horses might be able to do all the movements within two years, but they need to learn to relax and become familiar with this difficult work before they can achieve fluency.

First year

During this year a good deal of lunging is helpful, for working without the rider the horse can learn to find its own balance, particularly at the trot and canter. The person who is lunging must be very conscious of the rhythm of the paces and must help the horse to balance by maintaining constant contact through the lunge rein. This is best achieved by walking a small circle rather than pivoting around one point. The aims of lunging work are to establish rhythm, elasticity of step, suppleness of the body and willingness to be controlled.

In ridden work the objects are to establish a consistent rhythm to the walk, trot and canter, to perform the transitions in and out of the walk, to teach the horse to accept contact with the bit and to remain in the same outline between walk and trot. (If the outline is lost during transitions in and out of canter this is acceptable at this

A canter pirouette performed in excellent manner by the individual Olympic gold medallist Christine Stückelberger. In dressage it is important to maintain the true canter (three-time gait) and not to spin around pivoting on one leg, which the horse tends to do naturally and is the easier method of turning as used in western riding and polo.

Anne-Grethe Jensen and Marzog, the international dressage champions from Denmark. They are renowned for their fluent work: Marzog is always eager to listen to his rider and appears to find the work easy and enjoyable. All these features are shown in this extended trot.

early stage, as long as the horse is obedient to the aids to change the pace.)

Second year

The horse is taught to go sideways as well as forwards, in travers, shoulder-in, half pass, first at the trot and then at the canter. At the walk it should learn to do half pirouettes and at both trot and canter to lengthen the strides a little, but only as much as can be achieved without losing the rhythm, fluency and outline. For the naturally talented horse flying changes at the canter may be started.

Third year

The flying changes need to be established, so that they are done not merely obediently but with quality. Sequence changes are started, progressing from a change every fourth or fifth stride down to every second stride. It is sometimes feasible to ask for changes every stride, but only two in succession.

Pirouettes at the canter may be started, but progressively from large ones (almost a small circle), gradually tighten-

Figs. 26, 27 Lateral movements in which the horse moves sideways as well as forwards. The diagrams (below) show on the left the travers (quarters in), centre the shoulder-in, and right the half pass, seen also illustrated (left).

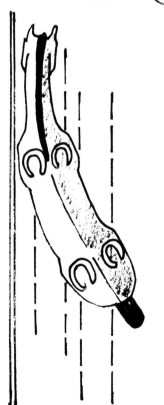
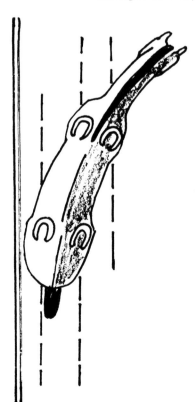
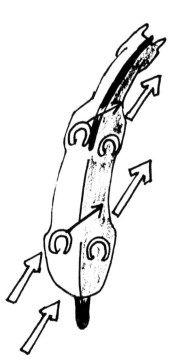

Fig. 28 The piaffe, a movement in which the horse trots on the spot, is only possible if the horse can achieve great collection.

Fig. 29 (right) The canter pirouette. In 6-8 strides of the canter the horse turns a complete circle of a radius equal to that of the horse itself.

ing up as the horse develops sufficient collection to turn in a smaller area while maintaining rhythm and fluency.

Throughout all the training more and more collection is gradually demanded and correspondingly more and more extension to the strides at the walk, trot and canter. Collection is not a separate movement but is developed by working on circles and movements, and at the same time the circles and movements will improve in quality as more and more collection is achieved. The vital factor to remember is that collection is not simply slowing down to make the strides shorter, for then much of the power is lost and the back stiffens; it is the shortening of the steps within the same rhythm, so that the steps become higher and more energy is contained within the horse.

Fourth year

All the changes should now be established, including the ability to change every stride (15 such changes are required in Grand Prix). The canter pirouettes need to be done as in the test, when the radius should be no more than that of the horse. Piaffe can be started, and passage is the last movement to be taught. If the horse has the ability to collect correctly, passage is achieved by simply allowing the horse to go forward out of the piaffe. There should be no great difference between piaffe and passage and those transitions between them will be easier.

The important point is that the training should be progressive, with more and more high quality collection being achieved, so that the movements come naturally to the horse. There should be no need to use force or cues to persuade a horse to perform, for if these are employed the movements become tricks rather than the natural outcome of the rider preparing the horse and putting it in such a position that the movement follows easily.

Fifth year

Once the horse has learnt all the movements the aim is to execute them with quality. The horse must be familiarized with all aspects of the test so that it remains relaxed and therefore able to maintain rhythm and work through the back, with softness in the jaw, straightness, regularity and – one hopes – brilliance of paces.

The Young Riders Champions of Europe, Renee Igelski and Baloo from Denmark, who perform a particularly good extended trot. They can achieve a pronounced moment of suspension, as in this picture.

The flying change at the canter, when the horse changes its leading legs during the moment of suspension. The horse, Angelino, is at present leading with the right foreleg (it is ahead of the other legs) but the rider, Jan Bemelmans, is about to ask for a change to the left.

The daily routine

All David Hunt's horses start with a ten to fifteen minute walk, preferably hacking, outside the arena. Then depending on their age and fitness they are given ten minutes' to one hour's work in the arena, followed by a five to fifteen minute walk. The young horses spend one day a week doing free forward exercise in the park, the older horses a little less often. All the horses have one day off a week.

FACILITIES

For serious work good going is essential. A sound footing helps the horse to be confident and relax. If the ground is slippery, constantly changing, or very hard the horse's tendency is to tense up and brace against the going. The strides will then become earthbound and that special lift and cadence which earmarks a good dressage horse will be lost. If the going is very deep the horse will have to struggle too much and will tend to lose forward momentum.

The ideal surface is one on which horses can freewheel. Some grass fields provide such a surface but rarely throughout the whole year, so more and more dressage riders now use artificial surfaces.

Some riders prefer an indoor school where bad weather can be ignored and the horses made to concentrate more easily. Outdoor arenas, however, have the advantage of familiarizing horses with some of the distractions they have to face in competitions. Although to have both is the ideal, David would prefer an outdoor arena if a choice has to be made. A full-size test arena (60 × 20 metres) is desirable as this makes it possible to practise all tests and easier to get the horse extending. In an area of this size the horse will have time to get into its stride, but a smaller arena of 40 × 20m is adequate.

EQUIPMENT

A good dressage saddle which fits both horse and rider is very important. Saddles which do not fit the horse can easily cause a sore back and hinder that vital working 'through'. Saddles which do not fit the rider or do not help him to establish a good position should also be avoided. For the rider to be effective he needs to acquire a classical position (Fig. 30), for only then will he be fully able to give the aids and keep in balance with the horse. A saddle should help not hinder the rider to acquire this position.

For the first two to three years, and during much of the training in later years, the horse can be worked in a snaffle bridle. The bit must fit and suit the horse: it should be of the correct width, and the type chosen – straight bar, jointed

Fig. 30 This horse is being ridden in a double bridle. The rider is sitting in a 'classical position' – an imaginary line would pass through his ear, shoulder, hip and the back of his heel.

with loose rings or eggbutt – according to which is most comfortable for the horse. The position of the teeth varies from horse to horse, and the animal will be much happier if a type of bit can be found which does not fall on its teeth.

The double bridle is usually introduced in the third year, but this timing will vary according to the horse. The trainer should be open-minded as to type, experimenting with different weights of bits, different lengths of cheek pieces, fixed or moving cheek pieces, loose or fixed ring snaffles. Most horses like room for their tongue to move around, so a bit with a port is usually best.

FEEDING

All David's horses are given hay ad lib, as he believes this keeps them relaxed and peaceful. Without food they often become irritable. It need not be the best quality hay because this is very high in protein and it is the roughage which is of value.

The hard food is varied according to the horses. Their basic diet is bran, flaked barley, oats, vitamin additives and occasional boiled feeds. The more advanced the horse is in its work, the more oats it can be given. It is usual for David's top horses to have 12-14 lb (5-6 kg) daily.

A great deal of food value is lost if the horse has to keep itself warm. Being warm also makes them happier, so David's horses have four or five rugs on them during the winter.

COMPETITIONS

Each rider will have a different level of competition as his goal. For David it is international competitions. He uses national competitions as preparation for international competitions, for they help to ensure that everything done at home is correct and of a high standard. They also help to familiarize both horse and rider with the trimmings of competitions, teaching them to relax when under pressure, for the horse must be supple and not tense if it is to show off the quality of its paces. Regular competitions put the rider under a little more pressure than if he is merely pursuing his own themes working at home. Also, the tests in dressage are designed to encourage the best type of training, so that it is not only the judges' comments which are of value but also having to train for and perform the different movements required in the test.

David plans his year by selecting shows where both the going and the facilities are good.

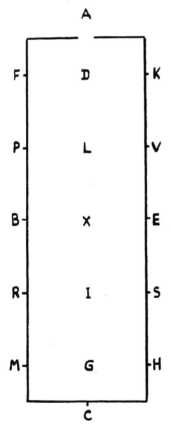

Fig. 31 An international dressage arena, 60 × 20 metres. The letters (which have no known significance) are those conventionally used to mark the positions for the various movements. At national levels a smaller arena (40 × 20 metres) is used and the markers P, R, S, V, I are removed.

The art of high class competitive riding is to be alert, to develop the craftsmanship to be able to ride accurate tests using the whole arena to show off the horse. Yet the rider must also be relaxed enough to do more than simply execute the movements (for then they are little more than circus tricks); they must be performed with quality whilst the natural brilliance of the paces is maintained.

This highlights one of the dangers in much dressage training. In the rush to compete at higher and higher levels, and in the trainer's desire to show off his ability, many horses are simply taught to do the movements. The natural quality of the paces is lost when making the horse go sideways, do flying changes, and attempt piaffe. Ability to do the movements is comparatively easy to achieve; what is much harder is to do them with that less definable quality which involves maintaining and enhancing the natural paces – to be able to go into high collection or extension whilst maintaining the same rhythm and brilliance to the pace. It takes many years for the horse to be able to cope physically and to understand what is required of it. The horse must learn to do everything upon the aids of the rider, for this removes the anticipation which creates the tension.

THE RIDER

For the horse's natural ability to be used to its full potential it must be well ridden. The successful dressage rider must be able to become totally involved physically and mentally with the horse. This involvement is rarely a natural talent and can be developed. The rider learns to carry on a conversation with the horse through the reins, to feel through his hands, seat and legs everything the horse is doing and about to do. He must learn to recognize problems and to solve them. A constant sensitive communication is thus established between horse and rider so that they become one unit capable of giving to each other.

To achieve this the rider must sit well so that he can remain in balance, give clear aids with his seat and legs, and feel what the horse is doing. He must be able to sit square and on the vertical so that he is able to relax, for tenseness in the rider hinders communication.

He should have an aptitude to learn and the dedication to do so. These attributes are more important than natural talent, for the gifted riders can be lazy and there is too much work involved in dressage to enable a lazy person to reach the top. The dressage rider must be, as David is himself, ambitious and willing to forgo other pleasures if he is to find out how to make the most of his horse's natural ability.

Show Jumping

Caroline Bradley

INTRODUCTION

Show jumping has the biggest worldwide following of any equestrian competition. More than forty countries are affiliated to the international ruling body, the Fédération Equestre Internationale (FEI), and in countries like Britain and Germany it is such a popular sport that television viewing ratings are close to those for football.

The appeal of show jumping as a spectator sport is due partly to the diversity and flamboyance of the characters at the top, and partly to the simplicity of the rules which make it much more understandable to the layman than driving, eventing or dressage, and produce an exciting climax to a competition with high fences and timed jump-offs.

The competitors jump a course of obstacles designed to test the horse's freedom, energy, skill and obedience in jumping, and the rider's horsemanship.

Competitors are penalized for mistakes over the course: 4 faults for a pole knocked down, 3 faults for the first refusal, 6 for the second, elimination for the third, 8 faults for a fall of horse or rider. In the case of the leaders having the same number of faults, either the fastest is the winner or there is a jump-off over a shortened course. If there is equality of faults in this jump-off, either the fastest wins or there is a second jump-off in which time is usually the deciding factor, although sometimes the prizes are divided between those with equal faults.

Besides these most common forms of competition – fastest clear round, one jump-off or two jump-off classes – there are numerous variations such as Puissance, in which

Fig. 32 A knockdown – 4 faults.

Fig. 33 A refusal – 3 faults.

Fig. 34 A fall – 8 faults.

competitors jump a wall which is built higher and higher each round so that height rather than speed is the determining factor. There are also many types of speed competitions in which seconds are added to the time if a fence is knocked down or extra points are earned by jumping the bigger fences, and knockout competitions with a pair of competitors racing against each other and the winner going through to the next round. Then there are team competitions, the most important being the Nations Cup (only one of which may be staged by any country each year), in which four competitors represent their nation, each jumps two rounds and the scores of the best three are added to find the winning nation.

Each of these different forms of show jumping competition demands a specialist type of horse. In high jumping, which calls for enormous scope and courage, the powerful German bred horses excel; for the timed class in which agility and speed are vital, the nippy little blood animals are usually best. The two- or three-round competitions with big courses and some fences set so that there are only one or two strides between them demand horses with a combination of these qualities – scope, courage and agility. They are the most highly valued show jumpers, for these are the competitions that determine all major championships. Every ambitious show jumping rider is looking for a horse capable of jumping such courses with ease. Very few horses will ever do so without exceptional natural ability that is recognizable in the very early stages of its career. Training appears to have less influence on the final quality of a show jumper than of other competition horses: it is much more difficult to change a good show jumper into a very good show jumper than it is to change the counterparts in eventing, dressage, polo or driving.

NATURAL TALENTS
The shape

Good conformation is important. The horse need not be beautiful (indeed the pretty types are rarely successful) but must be well made and well proportioned, for then it will usually be more balanced and therefore easier to work and less likely to have training problems.

The horse can be almost any type or height as long as its proportions are harmonious – for example, if it is chunky in front then it should be chunky behind. No particular type is supreme and successful show jumpers come in many different shapes and sizes. Caroline Bradley had top half-breds, Continental warmbloods and thoroughbreds; all can be great show jumpers if they have the other necessary attributes. With her sympathetic riding Caroline had greater success with thoroughbreds than most riders. She was particularly keen on them, although she found it difficult to acquire the right type at a reasonable price. In Britain thoroughbreds with a good jump, conformation, action and temperament are valuable steeplechase horses and way beyond the price-range of most show jumpers.

Action

The movement is easiest to cope with if it is unexceptional. The extravagant movers are usually difficult to contain at the canter, and the free paces of the event horses are also difficult as it is hard to teach such a horse to take the small bouncy strides required by a show jumper. The 'daisy-cutters', those with strides that have great swing and length but no lift or roundness, are similarly a problem. At the other extreme a horse with extra short strides usually lacks scope.

The normal unspectacular movers, besides being easiest to manage, also tend to have more natural balance which facilitates training and jumping high fences.

Of all the gaits the walk is probably most indicative of ability in the young horse. If this is good, showing suppleness and scope, it is likely that the horse will trot and canter effectively. Most talented jumpers have a good walk.

The vital factor with regard to all the gaits is that the hind legs should naturally come well under the body and that they should be used actively ('well oiled' hind legs). It is the hind legs which provide the power.

The front legs need to move freely. For this reason one should be wary of horses that swing their front legs (dish) and do not move straight, as this usually means that they

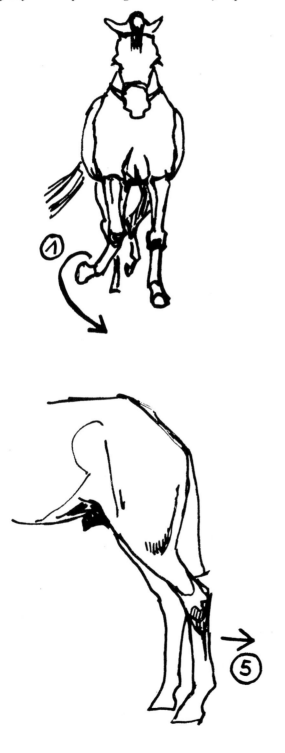

Fig. 35 Shortcomings that will hinder a horse's ability to jump easily and with style. (1) 'dishing', the foreleg swinging outwards as well as backwards and forwards. The horse has (2) a very straight shoulder, (3) a short neck badly set on, with more muscle underneath than above, and (4) a thick jowel. (5) these hindquarters will lack power as the hind legs are placed far behind.

Left, above: A young horse showing very good action when worked over trotting poles by Michael Saywell. The joints are well flexed and the outline is rounded, which will help develop the muscles the horse needs to jump in good style.

Left, below: A practice jump before a round in the arena. The rider has placed the horse close to the fence so that it will have to try hard and will have to bend its body to clear the fence. This is a good suppling exercise.

Loose jumping is a good means of evaluating a young horse's potential and of training it to look after itself rather than relying on assistance from the rider. Few horses, however, will jump naturally without encouragement and direction from a trainer on the ground. This horse is showing good style, having folded its forelegs, basculed (rounded its back and neck) and sprung off its hind legs.

Fig. 36 The approach to the fence. The horse is balanced with its outline rounded and the hind legs well engaged, qualities which will help it to jump with style.

are cramped in the shoulder and the freedom of the forehand is therefore restricted.

The show jumper must have balanced and powerful movements on the flat for this will help its approach and lift over the fences. The vital factor, however, is the way it jumps. However high a horse jumps, if the movement is unnatural the horse is unlikely to make the grade.

The horse should naturally look at the fence rather than hurl itself towards it. It should appear to lift off the ground effortlessly and with elasticity. The hocks should come well underneath the body during take-off and the shoulders should lift easily. The body should be under control so that the horse can push itself over with a natural rhythm and in a rounded outline, using the whole of the body and not just one section. Good conformation helps to achieve these actions.

Temperament

Character is vital. The show jumper has to be able to stand the pressure of top competitions, which involves accepting deafening noises and an electric atmosphere, and having the ability to relax and go quietly again after jumping flat out against the clock.

Fig. 37 A good style over the fence. The horse appears very athletic and the limbs are bent neatly. It is also basculing well.

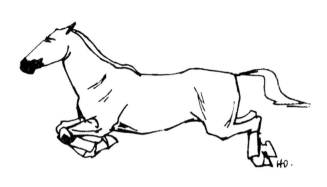

Fig. 38 Examples of poor style. With the back hollowed rather than rounded the horse (above) stiffens and will have to jump higher to clear the fence than the horse in Fig. 37. A horse with 'dangling' forelegs like the one (right) will have to jump relatively higher to clear a fence than the horse with folded forelegs.

The type of temperament can vary, the important factor being that it suits the rider. A sensitive rider can cope with a spirited horse, but such a rider might be hopeless on a lazier horse which needs great discipline, in which case a stronger, less delicate rider would cope better. There have been many great horses and great riders which have failed to make great partnerships. Horse and rider must suit each other both mentally and physically, and developing such an understanding between horse and rider is more important in show jumping than in other types of competition.

Although a show jumper has to stand up to considerable pressure, a docile well-behaved horse is rarely a great success. A horse that shows some signs of temper tends to dislike hitting fences; if it gets upset over any dislodged poles, it will try harder to clear future obstacles.

Many good horses are a little 'daft' as these horses tend to have the sharper reactions helpful in show jumping. They can look after themselves better if they are alert and quick-thinking. The daftness must not extend to going crazy under pressure or trying to get away from the rider by speeding up or hanging back. The horse must respond to the rider, and not be in front, behind, or unaware of him.

Assessing a horse's temperament, and especially how it will react under pressure, is difficult. The prospective horse can be ridden to a fence and pressure applied on the approach to see if it panics or tries to 'hurdle' it (jump it flat out with a straight or hollow back). A little can also be learnt from the horse's outlook, his head and his eyes.

CHANGES THROUGH TRAINING

Show jumping, which is probably the least natural equestrian sport – a horse is practically never seen jumping a fence in the wild of its own accord – is one in which very few changes are made to the horse's natural state to achieve peak ability in competitions. It does develop muscles, but these are neither as large as those of the dressage horse nor as hard as those of the eventer. It is made fitter, but not to the extent of the eventer or racehorse. The greatest changes are made to its movement. The canter, in particular, is brought under control, so that it becomes more balanced and powerful and responsive to the rider's demands to change the length of stride during the approach to the fence and after landing. But for most show jumpers these changes are at a fairly basic level of training and not very many hours are spent achieving them.

The horse's jumping ability is developed as far as possible, but it will probably be able to jump very little higher than when untrained. The improvements are made to its confidence so that it will jump many more types of obstacles, and to its balance so that it can jump consecutive fences, especially when these are at distances which require adjustment to the length of strides in order to arrive at the correct take-off point.

The major reason for relatively few changes being made to the show jumper is that such changes demand obedience. Many show jumping riders fear that obedience can

In these pictures (from right to left) the young horse is jumping a grid, a series of fences with no more than two strides between them. The horse shows great talent, clearing these fences with ease and obvious enjoyment, as can be seen from its pricked ears. The rider is sitting quietly, remaining in balance but not interfering so that the horse learns to look after itself and develop its style and athleticism.

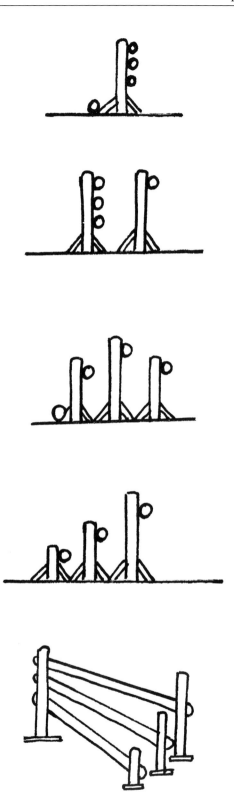

Fig. 39 The main types of show jumping fences. The top fence is an upright, the remainder are known as spreads. The most often used is (2) the parallel, then there are (3) the hog's back, (4) the triple bar and (5) the fan fence.

only be achieved at the cost of making the horses totally subservient to the rider, thus suppressing their spark and their eagerness to clear the fences.

Traditionally a very large part of the training simply entailed gaining experience at competitions. The importance today, however, of being able to jump a course even $\frac{1}{10}$ second faster than another competitor means that to save time sometimes only one or two strides are taken before a fence. Consequently corners have to be turned in a balanced fashion, and most riders find that some basic work on the flat does help to achieve this.

The extent of the changes attempted through training for show jumping varies somewhat, and some nationalities, the Germans in particular, train their horses to a much higher level of dressage and aim to exact greater obedience. Caroline represented the middle school, training her horses more than many British riders but less than the typical German.

TRAINING
Analysing the horse

The horse needs to be studied physically and mentally, so that its weakness may be clarified and worked upon. If, for example, it has a straight shoulder with restricted action it must be given flat work to free the shoulder. If the action is more powerful behind than in front, basic work is needed to lift the shoulders and to teach it to accept the bit (see page 41), otherwise the hindquarters will push downwards rather than upwards and such a horse will feel very heavy in the hands.

The good show jumping rider must also be capable of analysing the horse's mind. He has to assess his horse's character so that he can have the necessary measure of control without destroying the spirit and that vital will to clear the fences. Some horses need sympathy and confidence, others discipline and encouragement; all will respond to tact and adjustments by the rider rather than suppression and the imposition of a set method of training.

The really good horses think for themselves and thus help the rider out of difficulties. At the same time they must be sufficiently obedient not to fight the rider's aids – to turn willingly, and to shorten or lengthen their strides at his command. The latter is particularly important, for the horse must take off at a distance from the fence that will make it as easy as possible to clear big obstacles (see Fig. 40). If it has not learnt to adjust its stride it will have to take off sometimes too far back, sometimes too close and occasionally, by chance, just right. The good rider and, to a lesser extent, the good horse, judges long before the fence

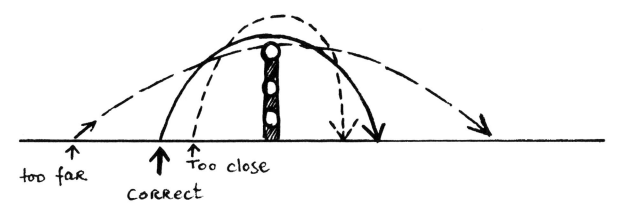

too far

correct

Too close

Fig. 40 The take-off point. The normal point (that is, the point from which it is easiest to clear the fence) is one and a half times the height of the fence in front of it. This rule does not apply to very high fences; over 1.5 metres the take-off point gets closer to the fence the higher it is.

where the best take-off point is, and by how much the strides should be lengthened, shortened or kept the same in order to arrive at that point. This ability to judge and then arrive at the best place to take off is a major skill in show jumping.

Caroline always tried to do the adjustments a good way from the fence so that she could leave the horse alone close to take-off. In this way the horse still feels in control, and thinks for itself. The key to this approach is that the horse respects the rider enough to obey, but the rider is sufficiently tactful for the horse to believe it is not dominated, and will consequently keep trying its hardest.

Way of going

The aim of the training is to enable the horse to make the best use of its natural ability to jump high and clean. Good training on the flat will make it easier for the horse to lift into the air. The manner in which it arrives at the take-off point can also be improved by training. The most important factor is balance, as this helps the horse to retain definite rhythm to its strides while approaching the fence, neither rushing nor slowing down. The centre of balance has to be adjusted backwards so that the natural manner of going, when the horse carries most of its weight on the forehand, is gradually changed so that more and more is carried on the hindquarters. By coming off the forehand the horse is able to lift off more easily, since the front becomes lighter (see Fig. 9 in the dressage section).

This balance should not depend upon the rider having to hold the horse together with the reins and legs; the horse must be capable of carrying itself in a balanced fashion without the rider's support (known as self balance). The horse must also learn to accept the bit (see page 40) in all

the work so that it is not wasting energy by fighting the rider or getting into a difficult take-off position through disobeying his commands.

More powerful canter strides can be developed if the horse uses its hind legs with great activity so that they can propel it more easily into the air. Each hind leg should be used equally so that the body is straight, otherwise much of this power will be lost (see page 40).

Fig. 41 This horse is resisting, which will make it hard for it to clear the fence. Not only is the horse wasting energy but its resistance will also necessarily stiffen the muscles thus reducing its athleticism. The back is not rounded and the hindlegs are not under its body, an outline which will inhibit the horse's power to spring.

One of show jumping's most famous combinations, Hugo Simon from Austria and Gladstone, seen turning a corner and obviously preparing to jump a fence. The horse is balanced and alert, and itself taking careful note of the fence ahead.

Liz Edgar and Forever, who have won major classes all over the world. This brilliant horse and rider have built up a tremendous rapport which makes them a great pleasure to watch. Note that both are concentrating and focused on to the next fence.

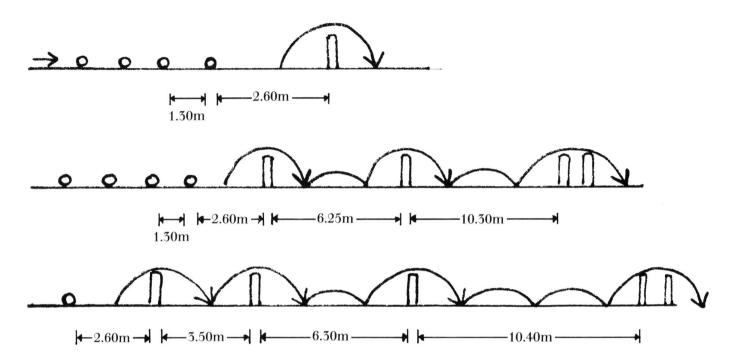

Fig. 42 Various grids used to increase the horse's gymnasticism. The horse trots into the series, but should break into the canter after the first fence; before the next fence it either bounces (no stride), or takes one or two strides according to the distance between the fences.

The jump

Jumping a fence either comes naturally to a horse or it does not. In the latter case the technique can be improved through skilful training on the flat, through grids (see Fig. 42) and over small fences, but the horse is unlikely to become a great show jumper. A horse with natural ability will not need to have its style adjusted but its athleticism and suppleness can be worked on so that it can make greater use of its body to jump high fences more easily.

Type of work

A special feature of Caroline's work was that she liked to train her horses in a low rounded outline (see Fig. 43), with their hindquarters tucked as far under as possible, and fully accepting the bit. In this manner of going the horse is using the same muscles (namely those along the back, especially behind the saddle, in the hindquarters and along the top line of the neck), as it does when in the air over a jump. If the head and neck are low and that light elastic contact is still maintained, the horse will have to use its shoulders, back and hindquarters.

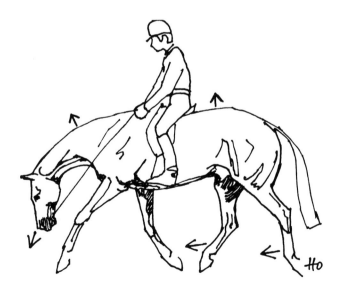

Fig. 43 This horse is working in the low rounded outline favoured by so many riders as a means of developing those vital muscles of the back just behind the saddle, as well as those in the neck and hindquarters.

Much of the work is done in this outline – the extending and shortening of strides, circling, slight bending of the body to one side then the other, going sideways, and riding on gently sloping hillsides. The purposes of the work on the flat are to make the horse supple, straight and responsive to the leg aids, both to go forward (legs used close to the girth) and to move the hindquarters sideways (one leg further back).

Trotting over poles and small fences

Caroline used to do a great deal of trotting over poles for she believed this gave her horses more interest and more work to do than on the flat. All the time, however, the same aims must be kept uppermost – accepting the bit, balance, rhythm, going forward but without rushing, power and, at the early stage at least, keeping the same low outline. When these aims can be maintained at a trot over the poles one may progress to very small fences, which are approached in the same way of going. Only when a fence of about 18 inches (45 cm) can be approached while maintaining all these aims is cantering started. The trot is established first because it is easier for a horse to keep its balance at this pace, and the horse should never be pushed beyond the speed at which it is balanced. A naturally balanced horse will progress through this trotting work easily and quickly, but this is not always an advantage. The longer time spent on the basic work with a difficult horse may mean that the work is better established and the horse will not have to rely so much on natural talent to get it over the fences in the future.

Still bearing in mind the maxims for the approach one may gradually attempt bigger fences, followed by doubles and trebles, and the gymnastic exercises of jumping grids (see Fig. 42).

The young horses progress to jumping whole courses before they attempt their first show. Unless there are problems, the jumping at home is reduced as the horse becomes more experienced and competes at higher levels. For the older horses, jumping at home consists of little more than a quick check-up to ensure every part of the body is bending and working as required, and a few gymnastic exercises to aid this harmonious functioning.

Hunting

Most of Caroline's horses were hunted before they started competing. It is good for their temperaments to learn to accept the excitements of the hunting field, and for them to learn in a 'fun' way how to jump ditches and other unusual fences. It makes them more mature and they usually progress far more quickly after a few days' hunting.

Horses which are naturally precocious and keen to go will not benefit from hunting, and it is not worth the risk of injury always present in hunting to include it in their training programme.

Varying the work

As the mental aspect of training a show jumper is so vital it is important to retain and encourage its co-operation and

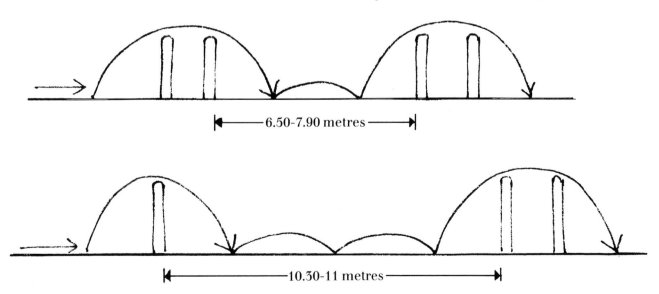

Fig. 44 A double of parallel bars (above) placed so that one stride can be taken between them. Below, a double of an upright in and a parallel out, with two strides to be taken between them.

The show jumping arena. An important aspect of training the show jumper is getting it used to the tremendous atmosphere created by big crowds and colourful, strongly lit arenas such as this.

The author of this chapter, the late Caroline Bradley, on her best horse, the Hanoverian Tigre. Caroline was respected throughout the world for her elegant, sympathetic riding which helped her horses to make the most of their natural ability.

Left: An excellent example of harmony between horse and rider: both appear relaxed but concentrating.

interest in the work. Consequently variety both of venue and type of work is beneficial. Caroline had an indoor and outdoor school, but she always tried to do much of the training while hacking out in the hills and the surrounding fields. Hill work is of special benefit as it encourages the use of muscles without the rider having to keep asking the horse to work correctly.

Most show jumpers get the occasional fast canter, but the amount of these given depends on the type of horse. Some horses physically need fast work to clear their wind, others which are on the lethargic side need to be very fit to make the most of their ability. Stuffy, lazy horses would therefore get plenty of cantering and gallops, but highly strung, forward-thinking horses might get very little.

TIME SCHEDULE

As with so many aspects of training a show jumper, there are no absolutes for the time schedule; again it depends on the character and physique of the horse and, much more than in any other equestrian sport, it must be adjusted accordingly, if best use is to be made of natural ability.

Some horses may need trotting over poles for six months, for although they may jump well they also find it difficult to maintain the necessary rhythm and balance on the approach; others may be cantering over fences within three weeks. But most types do tend to level out in the end, with different stages in the training taking longer for different horses. A brilliant jumper may be very spooky and take time to gain confidence. Another with great balance might progress very quickly, but its keenness may be destroyed if it is put under too much pressure before it has matured physically. Caroline always liked to turn such horses out to grass for frequent rests.

Caroline aimed to start training her horses as 3½- to 4-year-olds. At this stage the emphasis is on teaching them to go forward, but she might have tried jumping them over small fences on the lunge. Depending on their type and size they would then be given a certain amount of rest and started again in preparation for mid- and late-winter indoor competitions. They would then get another rest, enjoying the benefits of spring grass before more shows in the autumn. The length of their rests will depend on how much drill was needed in the training and competing. If they had to be worked very hard they are given more time to recover, but the usual break lasts about six weeks.

The first experience in the ring is normally as five-year-olds. This first competitive season is spent in the novice classes, the next in the middle grades, and by the time the horses are seven, they should be in the top national grades.

Their peak age varies according to type. The thoroughbred and lighter types take longer to settle and relax, and their best years are usually between 11 and 13. The Continental warmbloods mature quicker, so that the rider can and should apply pressure at an earlier stage. These types are at their best at around 8 to 10 years old.

Caroline's jumpers always got two rests a year if everything had gone according to plan and there were no enforced rests through injury. The timing of the breaks would depend on whether the horse was an international star, a second-line international, national Grade A, middle grade, or novice. Caroline had collected such a large number of talented horses that she had representatives in most of these leagues, so was herself competing year round (except for a Christmas, New Year break), and had different horses fit for competitions at different times.

The normal plan is a six week rest, then six weeks of fittening work followed by three months of competitions, this pattern being repeated twice a year.

Once in their competitive lives Caroline thought it a good idea to give the horses a longer rest of six months, as this refreshes them mentally and helps them to cope with the strain of top competitions and keep on enjoying them. This is best given once they are established, when they know enough to jump big courses at speed. By this stage the partnership will have been cemented and there will be an understanding which enables the rider to 'play' with the horse, the horse in turn co-operating and helping in the competition for fast clear times. A horse which has not thoroughly learnt the rules of show jumping, which does not listen to its rider, will usually have to be partially retrained after such a rest. An older horse, on the other hand, will lose a great deal of muscle and take a very long time to get fit again. Consequently it is the middle-aged, established horses which Caroline believed would most benefit from one long break.

FEEDING

The feed for show jumpers varies according to their characters and type. Some need as many oats as a racehorse, the more spirited and highly bred are best with no oats and a less energizing diet of nuts. The horses must feel very well, for the state of mind of wanting to clear fences is not a natural one. To achieve the necessary condition some will need to be very fit, others only half fit. The skill is to recognize the signs, to understand the character of the horse, and to vary the feed accordingly.

Show jumpers need to be fit in terms of muscularity, and must be fed accordingly, but they do not have to be galloping fit like a racehorse or eventer.

FACILITIES

The horses have to be jumped and worked at home, so poles and fences are needed, and the ground on which they are worked is most beneficial to their training if it is neither too deep nor too hard. Although well-drained grass fields are adequate for much of the time, if the training is to be continued all the year round, an indoor or artificial outdoor arena is needed.

COMPETITIONS

Arena practice plays a more important part in the training of a show jumper than of any other sporting equine. The conditions of a show cannot be recreated at home, so it is vital that horse and rider have plenty of opportunity at every stage in their career to get used to the atmosphere, colour and pressure of competitions, especially jumping against the clock. They must learn to excel in these conditions, not simply tolerate them.

A show jumper may therefore compete as many as four days a week, and this persistent experience will help to settle it in the work. This frequency does not put the horse under undue strain, because with only about two minutes in the ring there is no test of stamina, except perhaps in the case of mature performers in some major competitions like the Jumping Derbies.

As the show jumping class is an important part of training, wise competitors often use it as such, concentrating more on the horse's way of going than on winning. Caroline was respected for her long term planning and she sacrificed many competitions with the future in mind.

The competitive campaign can be planned for each horse, with shows being selected that will help to progress a particular horse for selected objectives.

Thus the type of course (flimsy, or strange and massive), the atmosphere (quiet or electric) and the ground (heavy, undulating, hard, good), will be appropriate for different horses at different times. The successful competitors are those who make careful plans.

THE RIDER

The more advanced stages of training for show jumping are done through the competition itself. The progressive build up to jump higher and more trickily sited fences and to do so in an increasingly lively and strong atmosphere is achieved through going to a large number of shows. To be a good trainer of show jumpers entails being a good competitor, especially in these advanced stages.

In the early stages horsemanship is needed, for the way of going is more important than clearing fences. The horse needs to learn to be balanced, and to retain its rhythm before, during and after the fence, to accept a measure of control without losing this balance, to allow its natural style to develop and to canter with power (the impulsion needed to jump). To achieve this, minimal interference as to where to take off (by lengthening or shortening the strides) is needed, whereas with the advanced horse such guidance is vital. Also the will to win, the key to competitive success, might have to be suppressed for it is harmful to try to win or to go fast against the clock before the horse is ready. Pushing the horse robs it of future achievements and takes years off its competitive life.

Consequently the skills needed for young show jumpers and the initial training are different to those needed at later stages. Some riders, of whom Caroline was an oustanding example, are able to adapt, but many top stars leave the early education of their horses to others.

To be able to train the horse in the later stages, mostly in the arena, the rider needs to be 'cool' when under pressure, before and during a class, to be a person who responds to the big occasion.

Flair for show jumping comes naturally to the great riders, but competence can often be achieved through dedication, determination and good horses. The vital quality is an 'eye' that enables the rider to judge far back from a fence where the horse should take off, so that he can ask the horse to adjust its stride accordingly. Judging the take-off point correctly makes it easier for the horse to clear the fence, and the further out the adjustments are made the easier it is to maintain rhythm and balance which helps the horse to go clear.

The other aspect of flair is having the timing and judgement to complete a good round against the clock – to know how fast the horse can go without losing its balance, how close it can be turned into a fence and still clear it.

Like their horses, show jumping riders benefit less from training than their counterparts in dressage, driving and eventing. Help may be needed at certain times, and in the early stages advice on style and working on the flat is particularly beneficial. But show jumping skills are improved more through determination, riding a good horse and competitive experience than by being told what to do.

Caroline is a prime example of this theory for she went to only one trainer – Lars Sederholm – and that only for a short period at the beginning of her career. She probably spent more hours in the show jumping arena in her all too short life than any other rider in the world.

Horse Trials

Richard Meade

INTRODUCTION

Horse trials are the all-round test of horse and rider. To be successful the horse must show obedience, suppleness and a correct way of going in the dressage; speed, stamina, courage and agility when going across country; and the ability and carefulness necessary for show jumping.

The three phases can be completed as a one-day event, but the ultimate in horse trials is the three-day event which is used in all major championships. For the most important three-day events the dressage is a medium level test in which the horses are not expected to show collection but they do have to extend, and complete lateral movements. The event horse, as opposed to the pure dressage horse, has an additional handicap in this phase as it has to be galloping fit and raring to go for the cross-country, and this makes it more difficult for it to relax in a dressage test.

The second phase, the cross-country, is the most influential on results, the most dramatic to watch and the most exhilarating to ride. The course may be anything up to 30 kilometres (18½ miles) and is divided into four sections: (A) roads and tracks, in which a specified number of miles have to be completed at 220 m per minute (a fast trot, or a combination of canter, trot and walk) and penalties are given for those over the time allowed. This is followed by (B) a steeplechase course over the birch fences on a racecourse or similar ground. Most horses have to go very nearly flat out if they are not to incur penalties, for the speed required is about 40 kph (25 mph). This section may

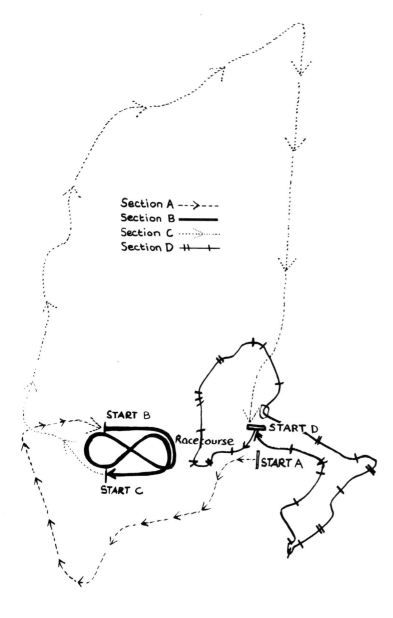

by cantering the last part. Then too there is a compulsory 10 minute halt before the most difficult section is started, (D) the cross-country.

The cross-country can be up to five miles long and contains between 30 and 35 obstacles. Although the fences cannot be higher than 3ft 11in (1.20 m) or wider than 5ft 11in (1.80 m) they are constructed in such devious and awe-inspiring ways that only horses which have been well trained to trust their rider, and to jump with boldness and dexterity, are likely to go clear.

A one-day event only includes section (D) of this phase, and it is shorter with smaller and fewer obstacles than in a three-day event. A two-day event can include all the sections, but these are a good deal shorter than in the three-day event.

After the great test for horse and rider of galloping at speed across country, competitors have to tackle a show jumping course. They must demonstrate that the horse has retained the suppleness, energy and obedience necessary to jump fences which might be small in comparison to international show jumping, but which are very difficult in view of the tests the horse has already completed, the lack of specialized training in show jumping and sometimes the great pressure on the rider if he knows that one fence down will cost him his present position, particularly if he is in the lead.

NATURAL TALENTS

The event horse must be an all-round athlete, for it is tested in all major forms of equestrian activities except driving. The ideal horse for eventing needs staying power and a good enough gallop to do the steeplechase without taking too much out of itself, but it need not be fast enough to win a race. Nor are most top show jumpers ideal for eventing, since their tendency to 'balloon' their fences – to jump very high and cleanly – means that they lose time in the air and are slow to accelerate away from the fences. Not even a Grand Prix dressage horse, however good its marks in the first phase might be, is suitable, for its high extravagant action is usually a limiting factor when galloping. What is needed is a good, consistent horse which performs proficiently in each of the sections; but excellence in one particular section is usually only achieved at the cost of other sections.

Shape

This all-round athlete must be very sound because eventing is a tough sport – as is the training – so any weaknesses are quickly exposed. The conformation needs to be correct

Fig. 45 The plan of the course for the second phase of a three-day event. Sections A and C are the longest but least testing as they need only be completed at a trot. Section B, the steeplechase, is the test of speed as competitors have to gallop over racing fences. They can recover on the second section of the roads and tracks (C) before the most spectacular section (D) which contains the cross-country obstacles.

exhaust some horses but they have a chance to recover as there is a second section of roads and tracks (C). The first part of this can be walked and often the riders dismount and run alongside their horses. The time can be made up

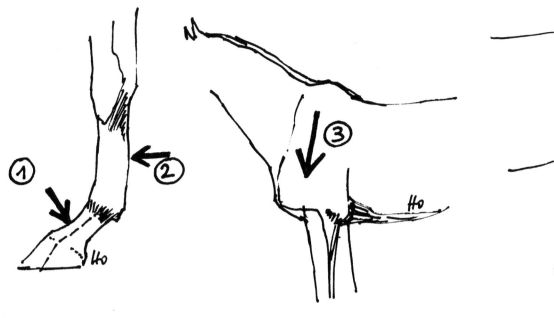

and well proportioned, for then no one area is subjected to excessive strain and the horse is more likely to remain sound. Another benefit of correct, well-proportioned conformation is that the horse is naturally balanced. The limbs need to be of good quality, with no obvious weaknesses such as bad hocks or weak tendons. The 'heart room' is important, that is the chest should be deep and broad, allowing plenty of room for the heart and lungs to operate and provide the horse with greater powers of endurance.

The shape of the shoulder is indicative of freedom of movement. If it is sloping and deep the horse usually has the freedom to move well in the dressage and gallop easily across country. The hindlegs, which should be neither straight nor sickle, must be powerful enough to propel the horse over such demanding fences as steps and jumps up hills.

The size of the horse is not crucial. A big horse tends to take longer to recover from injury and has to develop great agility to tackle the awkward fences, but the longer legs are an advantage in helping to balance it when jumping the water.

The type of horse is important. The thoroughbred is popular, but it needs plenty of bone and substance for the horse to stand up to the tough tests, and care must be taken that it has a good temperament as so many thoroughbreds are less reliable than the commoner types.

Conversely if a less refined breed or type is chosen it must have great quality, as well as being sufficiently fast not to be under constant pressure to complete the times on the steeplechase or across country.

Fig. 46 Various deficiencies in the shape of an eventer: (1) a long sloping pastern, (2) a weak tendon, (3) a straight shoulder, (4) a weak straight hock, (5) a straight hind leg, (6) a sickle hock and (7) a curb.

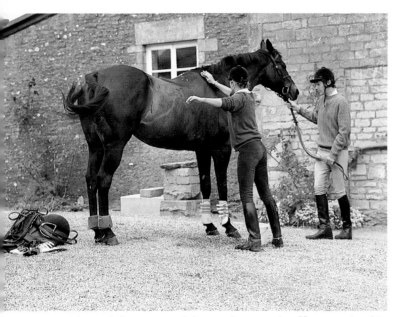

A horse being sponged down after exercise. Horsemastership – care of the horse when not being ridden – is a vital aspect of preparing an eventer. To keep the horse sound and at peak fitness tremendous care has to be taken over cleanliness, health, feed and environment.

Richard Meade training for the dressage phase at home in an artificial arena. A peaceful atmosphere such as this will increase the horse's concentration and its ability to learn.

Right: Richard cantering his horse up an incline. Riding 'upsides' helps to make the horses keen and ready to go faster if required.

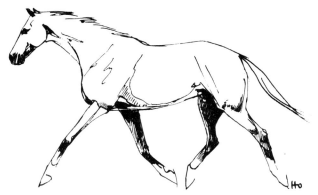

Fig. 47 A good trot for an eventer, showing plenty of freedom, good use of the shoulders and hindquarters, but not so much suspension and potential to collect (shorten and elevate the strides) as a dressage horse.

Action

An event horse should move straight, since any swings, dishes and the like in its action tend to restrict the gallop and put added strain on to joints, ligaments and tendons. The sport itself places so much strain on the horses that any additional pressures should be avoided.

The paces should be correct and good enough to help the horse earn points in the dressage. The important factor, however, is the horse's ability to take free sweeping strides. A rounded springy action is less important in the dressage as collection is not demanded, and across country it is a handicap as it will prevent the horse galloping economically. The easier it is for the horse to gallop with speed, the less it has to be pushed on the cross-country course, and this in turn reduces the chances of injury.

It is difficult to judge how good a gallop the young horse will develop, for this pace cannot be tested until the horse is fit and mature. The walk is indicative, however; if the young horse takes long swinging strides at the slowest pace, the prospects for the fastest are good.

Temperament

A sensible temperament is important, for the event horse has to be very fit when it is ridden in a dressage test. One way of testing this is in the hunting field. Any horse which becomes hot tempered and scatty when following hounds is unlikely to make a top-class eventer. When you cannot use this means of character assessment, you should consider the horse's type of head and eye and its pedigree. If it is out of a sensible mare and by a sire with equally tempered progeny, the chances of it also having a good temperament are increased.

The temperament should be generous too, as it is vital that the horse tries his best when faced with the hazards of the cross-country. Again this is a quality difficult to test, but the horse's eye offers some indication, and the manner in which it tackles strange obstacles, however small, helps the assessment.

It is preferable for a young horse to be lethargic rather than too hot-headed. Usually as a horse gets stronger it becomes more alert, but a scatty horse, however talented, is likely to be unreliable and usually lets the rider down when under pressure.

In dressage and driving the indefinable vital extra needed for top-class performance is 'presence'. In eventing it is 'class'. This can perhaps best be illustrated through a comparison with cars. A car which is driven continuously flat out on a journey eventually packs up, but the more 'classy' model which does not need to be driven at full capacity will continue for much longer without problems. The eventer too must have quality to cope with the time limits on the cross-country without having to be at full stretch.

Breeding is the major determinant of class. Although the odd touch of common blood helps the temperament, some well-bred refined ancestors, of proven ability over long distances, are needed to provide the 'staying' blood.

CHANGES THROUGH TRAINING

The eventer's training is midway between that of a racehorse and a dressage horse, and so is its appearance. Thus it is not as lean and wiry as a racehorse, yet to avoid the strain of extra weight on limbs and wind and to enable it to gallop, the eventer has less covering than a dressage horse. Some of the muscles seen on dressage horses do develop on the eventer, particularly those on the neck and back, but not to such an extent for there is very little collected work included in the eventer's training.

A major change that occurs to the event horse during training is in its fitness – the most complete all-round fitness found in a horse. The lung and heart capacity is increased to give greater powers of endurance, muscles are developed to help galloping, jumping and performing dressage.

The scope of the horse's movement is increased, enabling it to take shorter and longer strides in balance at the walk, trot, canter and gallop than it did naturally. The emphasis is on changing the size of the stride, so it does not matter too much if the event horse learns to shorten without true collection, for although dressage-type collection is the ideal the training involved is time-consuming and difficult for the horse bred and trained to gallop.

The gallop will have to be developed, but in a different way to that of the racehorse. Care has to be taken that the eventer's balance is not too far forward so that it can lengthen and shorten its strides at speed and jump the fences cleanly and accurately.

The event horse's character should become more relaxed with training so that it is happy in its work and capable of maximizing its ability. The riding, feed and handling are all directed towards this end.

TRAINING
Trust and obedience

For an event horse to take on these difficult cross-country courses it must have great trust in its rider and confidence in its own ability. The central theme of training is to develop such qualities and the major contributory factor towards their achievement is that the horse should understand its rider's aids and orders, and obey them.

The horse obeys because it trusts that its rider will not ask the impossible, and occasionally the rider will have to convince the horse of this by being tough if it refuses. Thus if a fence is frightening, strong aids may have to be applied to get over, but if the pupil gets over without hurting itself, its trust will increase. If on the other hand it is allowed to refuse, it loses respect for its rider, and all too often refusal becomes a habit.

Fig. 48 A fit eventer, carrying more weight and muscle than a racehorse but less than a jumper or dressage horse.

Fig. 49 One of the important changes in the training of an eventer is to teach it to shorten and lengthen its stride without wasting its energy and creating tension through resisting its rider's aids.

Left: Horse trials can be dangerous. Falls like this do occur but it is surprising how rarely they damage horse or rider physically. Often much more serious is the psychological damage to confidence which is a vital aspect of success in eventing.

This horse is showing great confidence and willingness to jump in the hands of its accomplished rider, Bruce Davidson from the United States.

Once a horse has learnt to stop and thinks this is an option when approaching a fence it rarely becomes a top eventer. Stopping, therefore, is to be avoided at all costs. Strong aids may have to be used when necessary to build up confidence and to avoid disobedience, and a horse should never be asked more than it has the ability to perform easily. If a horse is scared of a particular type of fence, let us say ditches, it is best to jump simple ones only to begin with so that the horse can clear them however reluctant it may be on the approach. If it does not hurt itself confidence will gradually increase, and with it the size and difficulty of the fences.

It is not just over fences that this trust is developed. Many horses want to go faster than the rider thinks is right. Richard believes that it is important to be firm, not passive, and insist that the horse goes in the way required. This develops confidence, for an experienced rider knows the speed at which it is easiest to do the work. Many horses rush fences through fear and lack of confidence rather than because they are keen to jump. This inevitably gets them into difficulties, for they eventually meet a fence wrong and hit it or fall, thus losing more confidence.

To gain confidence the onward going horse must go at the speed the rider requires, on the flat and over fences, even if this means using a strong bit until it has learnt the lesson. The lazy horse on the other hand may have to be encouraged to go faster if it tries to go slower than the speed required by the rider.

Increasing the athleticism

Developing athleticism is the main aim when training an event horse. Most of the work – the jumping, the grid work, the dressage, the hill work – if done correctly will help towards this end, but another exercise that Richard finds particularly useful is shortening and lengthening the horses' strides. During flat work, when hacking, even when doing fast work and cantering in a jumping position, he will ask the horse to shorten and lengthen his strides frequently. The ability to extend and shorten at all paces makes a horse more powerful, supple and agile – and, of course, more controllable.

Way of going

Throughout all the work, whether it is in the arena, on roads, up and down hills or galloping, Richard likes his horses to work correctly, in the same manner of going as in a dressage test. The paces may be different and the balance different but there must be consistency. If the rider always

asks for acceptance of the bit (see page 41), a good balance and correct transitions these become deeply ingrained into the horse's way of going. Conversely, if the horse is allowed too much freedom on a loose rein it tends to fall on to its forehand and stop using itself efficiently. Correct work at all times helps to make the horse more supple, to develop the right muscles, and even aids mental relaxation, for once the discipline is accepted it can be understood, whereas spasmodic freedom is often hard to cope with.

Condition

The heavy demands of eventing make keeping a horse sound and in good condition an important aspect of training. Basic veterinary knowledge is helpful, as this makes it possible to recognize warning signs so that the training can be eased or interrupted in time to stop a serious problem developing.

Horses have to be in good condition if they are to give their best. The eventing season is long, so Richard likes the horse's body to be well covered yet not so much that its ribs cannot be felt. Too much body weight puts more stress on the horse's legs and respiration, but too little can put an end to its competing. If a horse starts to lose weight (to run up light), or has been doing incorrect work and developed the wrong muscles – for example, those under rather than on top of the neck – Richard likes to take it out of work. Such a horse can be rested and let down, its condition softened before building it up again and through correct work developing the correct muscles.

Fig. 50 Allowing the horse to walk in this way, when so much weight is on the forehand and the back is hollowed, will not develop the correct muscles nor will it help the horse to achieve a beneficial way of going.

Fig. 51 This horse is very thin and has more muscles on the underside of its neck than the topside. Such a horse will be difficult to train and should be given a rest.

The all-round athlete

In the three-day event there are five different phases for which to train, but it is important to try to be as consistent as possible in all of them, to ask for the same manner of going at all times.

It is important too that each phase is given sufficient attention. If a horse is poor at dressage it is usually a mistake to spend most of the training time on this phase, for however much this improves its marks in that particular section, the others are likely to suffer. The event horse must be trained as a whole. The art of training for the three-day event is to tune the horse up for all five phases.

Dressage

The event horse is trained for this first phase of the horse trials in much the same way as a dressage horse in its first and second year, but as the other phases have also to be worked on, less time can be spent in the dressage arena. The rate of progress can afford to be slower, however, since the objective for the event horse is medium level work and this is not required until participating in the top three-day events, so there should be at least three years in which to train for this standard.

The standard of the medium level dressage at top three-day events is very high. This is partly because the best horses will have been working on the same test for a number of years, and partly because top riders are aware that the dressage is very important. The leader at the dressage phase is more and more often the winner of the overall event, and competitors are realizing that they must give themselves, as well as their horses, a great deal of dressage training if they are to win horse trials.

Training for dressage also has the added attraction of developing obedience, suppleness and rhythm, assets which can be applied with benefit in all the other phases of the competition.

Jumping

It is important for the event horse to learn to jump at a speed at which it can see and judge what it is tackling. If it starts by hurrying and trying to get to the other side as quickly as possible, it will run into problems with bigger fences: meeting an obstacle at the right take-off point to enable it to get to the other side will then become largely a matter of luck. Also, relying on speed to get over fences usually entails a flat style of jumping.

An event horse must learn to use its body, to jump with a rounded outline (bascule), which is the most efficient way of jumping and the safest method of tackling tricky obstacles. Thus Richard likes to jump all the fences very slowly and quietly at novice levels, and although the ultimate object is to gallop at the fences he only introduces speed when the horse has found its balance and a good style.

The horse learns to jump by trotting over very small single fences and grids, a series of poles and small fences with the distances between them carefully arranged to make the horse bounce, or take one or two strides (Fig. 53). The distances can be set so that the horse has to jump slowly, and is not able to speed up and hollow his outline over the fences. As training to help teach the horse to shorten and lengthen his strides progresses, the distances between the fences in the grid are adjusted so that on some occasions the horse has to take short strides down the line, and on others long strides. Bounces – two fences with no stride in between – can be introduced, and some fences progressively approached at sharper and sharper angles, in preparation for the angled fences in horse trials where it is necessary to save time by cutting corners and jumping off turns. The aims in all this work are for the horse to keep a rhythm on the approach and to round its outline over the fence.

The bascule should not be too pronounced, however, as the fences are negotiated at a faster pace than in show jumping and if the horse jumps very high and round and lands steeply after the fence it will lose time in the air and accelerate slowly away from it. The obstacles are not as high as show jumps and the important factor is that the event horse jumps freely. This means being able to 'stand back', or take off far from the fence. Thus show jumping training, when the rider consistently places the horse at a

The roads and tracks section of the cross-country phase. The competitors must complete this section in a specified time but it can be achieved by going at a good trot.

A cross-country course presents a great variety of obstacles, not all of which entail springing into the air. This is a slide which the horse and rider are completing with good balance.

Fig. 52 A horse jumping in good style for horse trials. It is not jumping very high in the air which means it is neither wasting time nor risking becoming unbalanced by the rough or sloping landings frequently found in eventing.

close take-off point to the fence, is inadvisable if this develops a ballooning, time-consuming style.

A horse which jumps its fences very big will run into problems across country, as again it will lose time in the air, and in tricky combinations where there is little space it might land far out from the fence and not be able to take off for the next section. Clever, agile jumping is what is needed, and big jumpers must be encouraged to develop a neater performance through grid work.

Grids can be used by adjusting the fences, poles and distances between them to develop attributes which are lacking in the horse's natural style of jumping, or to restrict those which are likely to create problems.

In eventing balanced careful landings are vital so that the horse is ready for anything immediately it touches down. It

has to be taught to land in a balanced fashion on slopes and different terrain, and to be able to change direction on landing. One way of stopping a horse from jumping too far out is to put a pole on the ground 3-3½ metres from the fence. The horse will soon learn that it has to get its feet down in front of the pole.

The show jumping phase of a three-day event is difficult to train for, as the major problems cannot be recreated. The course itself is easy compared to a show jumping course, and it does not take long to teach a horse to clear these relatively small fences. The problem is that the fences are designed to fall easily to incur penalties, and in a three-day event the horses have been galloping at massive permanent fences the day before. The show jumps, in contrast, create no great natural urge in the horse to clear them; they demand a much more rounded style which is particularly difficult for the horses when they are probably stiff and tired after the gruelling cross-country. And to make matters worse the rider is usually pretty tense, since so much hangs on jumping what are, in the circumstances, very difficult fences to clear.

Cross-country

It should now be clear that there are some differences between the style needed for show jumping (careful, rounded and very accurate), and that demanded across country (bold, free and fast). The initial training, described above, is the same for both; it is only when the speed element is introduced that the styles begin to differ, and most top riders leave this until a very late stage in their training, as speed hinders agility, relaxation, rhythm and balance. Only the well-trained horse can cope with achieving these demands at speed without regressing in its training and losing these attributes.

For both show jumping and cross-country one of the most important factors is to encourage the horse to enjoy its jumping, and one of the best ways of achieving this is by

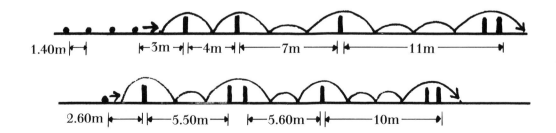

Fig. 53 Useful grids for eventers. The top line has distances for which the horse must take long strides; in the bottom line   *the grid is set to encourage short strides.*

hunting. It is a sport which horses respond to quickly: their natural herd instinct makes them want to go with the other followers and they quickly identify jumping fences with getting to the hounds, and identify hounds with providing excitement. It is a stimulating, exhilarating and natural pastime for horses and one which develops their desire to get over fences. The only trouble is that this desire often becomes over-developed and they want to get there too quickly. If the horse is immediately impetuous, or becomes so after a while, it is best to keep him at the back of the followers. The usual hazards of hunting, such as kicks from other horses, falls and getting caught in wire, have to be faced as well, so it is an unnecessary risk to hunt experienced horses. Richard only takes out the novices; an experienced eventer should no longer be in need of this form of training.

Apart from the benefit of the naturalness of hunting as a form of training, it also teaches the horses to cope with different goings, and with ill-defined take-offs and landings before and after strange obstacles. The horse can learn how to look after itself and how to make that extra effort when tired.

Hunting is also good for the rider, helping to develop his horsemanship and to give him the experience of riding a tired horse and learning how to conserve its energy.

For those who have no access to hunting, the experience it gives has to be created at home. This means that many more and different types of cross-country fences will have to be found (or built) and jumped. Practising over those behind or beside another horse is a step towards developing the herd instinct provided for in hunting.

Even the horse which has been well hunted will need to practise over the many types of cross-country fences, as only a few are found in the hunting field. They can be very small, miniature versions, so that the horse can be trotted into them and will have time to size up the fences. Event horses must learn as well to cope with such added dimensions as jumping obstacles going up and coming down hills.

Cross-country training continues at the events themselves. At competitions the gallops between fences and at the approaches to fences can be made at a progressively faster and faster pace, but the rate will depend on how well the horse is achieving the objectives of rhythm and balance, which are best learnt going slowly.

Richard's ultimate goal in jumping cross-country is that when galloping towards a fence he can set his horse up for that fence by bringing his centre of gravity back slightly, closing his hands, and 'asking' with his legs. This should be

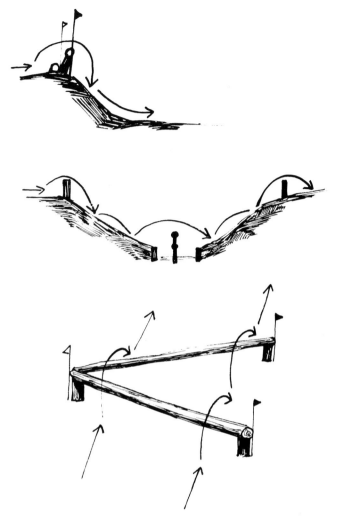

Fig. 54 Various types of fences found on the cross-country – the drop (top), the coffin and the corner fence. The bold would take this to the left but would have to clear a big spread and risk a run out; the cautious take it to the right as a bounce.

enough to create more impulsion, and to draw the balance back so that it is easier to adjust the stride if necessary and the horse is freer in front to lift over the fence. This action should be barely noticeable to the observer. Although this is Richard's objective in training it requires such great obedience, suppleness, rhythm and balance that he has only been able to achieve it to his satisfaction with four of his horses.

The ability to make these fine adjustments, to be able to measure up each fence without losing rhythm and balance, requires great mental and physical communication between horse and rider. It makes for a much safer ride across country and for a much longer competitive life for the

Richard Meade takes his horse through the first phase of the horse trials, dressage. Though perhaps less exciting than the other phases it is no less important, demanding different qualities of precision, control and elegance.

The final phase – show jumping. The fences may be smaller than in pure show jumping but they are still very difficult to clear on horses which are tired and stiff after a gruelling cross-country. Richard Meade and Bleak Hills clear this one in grand style at the World Championships staged at Lexington, Kentucky, USA.

horse than just galloping at the fences and relying on luck.

Endurance

Without the fitness to endure the length of the cross-country, no amount of jumping ability will get a horse over the fences. One of the best ways of achieving fitness is hillwork. This develops the muscles, particularly those vital ones behind the saddle, and ensures that the heart and lungs work hard but with much less strain on the forelegs (the most vulnerable part of the horse) than galloping on the flat. The three-day event is very tough, so training should exert the minimum wear and tear on the horse.

Cantering up hills helps fitness and muscles, walking or trotting slowly down them correctly (with the horse accepting the bit and so on) helps the horse to compress its frame, use its hindquarters and arch its back – all great benefits in training.

The hills must be used with discretion, the speeds and number of times climbed depending on the hill's steepness and length and the age and fitness of the horse. A four-year-old might only trot up once, whereas a horse nearly fit for a three-day event might canter up three or four times.

Speed

Horses have to be trained to gallop in balance when carrying the weight of the rider. To achieve this it is best to

Fig. 55 An eventer galloping. Although perhaps not so fast as a racehorse it is showing good use of the hindlegs, which are the source of power to clear fences and will help the horse to keep balanced over rough terrain.

keep them at no more than three-quarters their maximum speed until they are competing in three-day events. A stuffy horse with a short stride, however, will need to be worked more strongly than a big, easy-striding horse which might need working quite slowly to keep it relaxed and in rhythm.

The horse which is reluctant, or not a natural galloper, must be given every encouragement such as galloping in the company of another horse to encourage it to try harder and enjoy the pace more. It is more natural for a horse to go fast if asked to do so on a straight line rather than a circle, and when training it is important to work out what is natural to the horse and to use this to bring out the best of its ability.

TIME SCHEDULE

A naturally able horse that has lost little time in training or competitions through injury or illness takes about four years to prepare for the top three-day events.

Richard hunts the horse if possible in its first year and does general basic training at home. In the second year he will enter it for some competitions, but usually only of Riding Club standard with the odd official Novice Trial being used for training rather than winning. He will sometimes include a summer season of show jumping as well. In the third year the official trials are attempted in earnest with a view to up-grading the horse. In the fourth year the pupil should be mature enough to gallop and develop its stamina, and experienced enough for medium dressage and the larger obstacles, so three-day events are then a possibility.

Once the horse has become a three-day eventer there is a fairly set pattern to its annual work. It is turned out in the fields to rest after the last autumn horse trial and brought into work about Christmas time. For five or six weeks it will be limited to road work, at first only at the walk but later the odd trot is introduced. This slow and fittening work on a firm surface hardens the limbs in preparation for the strains ahead, and ensures that the condition gained in the field is not lost by sudden exercise.

From around the fifth week schooling starts, with a little daily dressage in the arena before hacking out. In the sixth week this dressage includes a good deal of canter work. Jumping over small fences and grids starts in the seventh week, as does the cantering up hills. Jumping starts in earnest after two months, for the schedule is to practise jumping for the three weeks prior to the first competition. This will be a one-day event, at least two and a half months after the rest ended. The fast work is then stepped up, another one-day event tried, and after three to three and a half months the horse should be nearing peak fitness and be ready for a three-day event.

Sometimes there will be more one- or two-day event before the three-day event, but straight after this ultimate test of a three-day eventer a short rest is usual. Not so much road work will be needed when the horses come in from the fields in summer, but the rest of the preparation is similar to that in the winter and early spring. Top horses then tackle their second three-day event of the season in late summer or early autumn.

The eventer enjoys longer rests than most types of horses but it needs them to unwind mentally and physically after its stamina has been tested, usually close to the limit, in a three-day event.

FACILITIES

Event horses need an arena in which dressage and jumping can be practised all year round. The better this ground is the greater it helps the development of natural movement and the athleticism for jumping. In England most serious riders have an artificial surface because the vagaries of the weather often make the fields too hard or too soft for much of the year.

There should be good facilities for fittening the horses, that is well-drained fields, hills if possible, tracks or roads which are safe for riding.

Access to cross-country fences, and a good variety of them, is essential. These should not be sited on ground that is too hard, as joints are easily strained in these conditions.

For galloping it is essential to have good ground because of the wear and tear done to the horses on hard, deep, rough or heavy going. Tendons are all too easily strained when galloping facilities are poor.

FEEDING

The three-day eventer has to be fed like a racehorse to maximize its energy and help it become an athlete in peak condition. This is difficult, as a horse at the peak of its fitness tends to become very fussy, and will not remain at the peak unless this fussiness is overcome and it eats well.

The feeding is graduated in the same way as the work. Thus in the early stages the oat ration is smaller and the hay ration larger. As the horse gets fitter the hard food is increased so that the food and work complement each other.

COMPETITIONS

The way in which competitions can be used depends on the standard of horse and rider. The top rider uses the one-day event as a means of training, helping the horse to relax in a competitive atmosphere, to get used to different types of cross-country fences, and so on. They are a means to the end of tackling a three-day event. Everything is geared to this end, so that all other forms of horse trials – one- and two-day events in the case of a young horse, or in the weeks prior to a three-day event – are rarely entered to win. For less able or less ambitious riders, any horse trial is an end in itself.

Event riders also use other forms of competition to help train for horse trials. Many young horses spend a few months show jumping, and practically all the eventers practise arena craftsmanship by entering pure dressage competitions.

THE RIDER

The attribute most needed by an event rider to change his horse into a top competition horse is an enjoyment and flair for cross-country riding. His horse has to trust him if it is to take on those fearsome obstacles, and to build such a trust it is essential to have balance, rhythm and a sense of timing. These qualities are usually natural to a rider but are open to improvement with training. They need to be combined with self-discipline for the horse can be injured or lose confidence through rider error – incorrect timing of a section, slap-happy walking of the course, misjudging speed. Dash and natural flair alone are not sufficient.

The cross-country is only one phase, however. The event rider must be interested enough in dressage to accept the training that will make himself and his horse competent at medium level. This again entails discipline, attention to detail and a keen interest in the challenge of improving the horse's way of going.

The rider has to help his equine partner and therefore be able himself to adapt to the different requirements of each phase. An important aspect of this, and one in which the horse has to rely on the rider, is the ability to develop different types of pace. The canter needed for show jumping is different from that for dressage and cross-country. The rider has to recognize the optimum pace for each phase and help his horse achieve it. This feel for pace is rarely natural but has to be developed through experience.

Richard, who is the world's most experienced event rider, is master of this feel for pace. His horses do not excel in one phase at the expense of others, but are trained and perform as all-round atheletes – the essence of three-day eventing.

Driving

Peter Munt

INTRODUCTION

Driving trials are the newest of the international equestrian sports. The rules for this three-day event on wheels were drawn up by the International Equestrian Federation (FEI) in 1969. A competitor may drive a single, pair or team (4 horses), but the international championships are only open to the latter as these require the most skill to control.

Driving trials are divided into dressage and presentation, the marathon, and obstacle driving. The dressage takes place in a 100×40 metre arena and the tests include changes of pace between collected, working and extended, the rein back, 20 metre circles, all of which are done at the walk or trot. Presentation is also judged at this phase. The aim is to maintain the traditions and elegance of carriage driving, thus the Whip (the person who drives the carriage), grooms, harness, horses and carriage are awarded marks for their turnout, cleanliness and correctness of equipment.

The second phase is the most exciting. The carriages are driven on a 24-30 km marathon, divided into sections which have to be completed in specified times otherwise penalties are incurred. There are sections which have to be walked, sections in which the horses should trot and, most difficult of all, the hazard section where competitors have to negotiate water and make difficult turns through trees, barrels or other man-made obstacles. It is in this section that carriages turn over, poles are broken, and horses even refuse to co-operate for the hazards are constructed to test the obedience and courage of the horses as well as the skills of the Whip.

The final phase is the obstacle course. This takes place in an arena which contains about 20 obstacles, each consisting of two rubber cones topped with small balls. If horse or carriage hits a cone the ball is dislodged, and penalties are incurred. Further faults are awarded if the competitor does not complete the course within a specified time.

The driving trials horse is therefore tested for its obedience and movement in the dressage arena, for endurance, courage and manoeuvrability in the marathon, and for suppleness, fitness and obedience in the obstacle phase. A successful driving horse must be an all-round athlete capable of doing well in each of these phases.

NATURAL TALENTS

Shape

A horse for driving trials needs to be strong and to have a good deal of 'bone' (circumference of the foreleg just below the knee). Fragile horses are not able to stand up to the rigours of competition or the lengthy exercise and schooling needed in preparation for the events.

The horse should be well put together, as this will help it to stay sound, and compact (between 15 and 16 hh), for if big or long-backed it will be difficult to manoeuvre through the obstacles.

The shoulder plays an important part in a driving horse as this provides the pulling power. (Note that in driving it is pulling power that counts, whereas in the other equestrian sports the emphasis is on pushing from the hindquarters.)

A good deep shoulder is useful, as is a harmonious connection between the wither and an arched neck.

If the hindquarters are rounded they will stand more weight than if they are sloping, and with extra muscle the horse looks and moves better.

A neat head not only looks more attractive, it usually means that the horse has a good temperament.

Temperament

Temperament is very important for driving horses since they have to remain calm when anything goes wrong, as it often does in competitions. If a carriage turns over they must not panic but should stand quietly, and similarly if a leg goes over a trace or a tree trunk is hit.

Yet to be a top-class driving horse that little extra – a certain 'presence' – is needed (see Fig. 12). Horses with such a quality take more skilful handling but they do earn the higher marks.

Action

The carriage horse is not required to canter; all the work should be done at the walk and trot, although to be fast enough through some of the hazards the occasional canter stride is taken. The walk is the important pace. The horses need to walk out really well when shown on a loose rein. It must be natural for them to cover the ground and be keen to go forward, for the walk section of the competition has to be completed in a fast time otherwise penalties are incurred. Little can be achieved by training to improve the

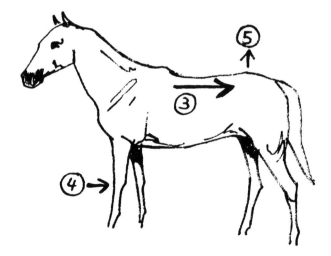

Fig. 56 Defects in a driving horse. (1) A short shoulder, (2) a badly set neck with a concave rather than convex top line, *(3) a long back, (4) back at the knee, (5) a straight croup which makes it difficult for the hindquarters to be rounded.*

walk and enable a horse to go at a faster speed because if a trainer asks a horse to walk faster, all that usually happens is that it takes quicker strides which tend to become shorter as it gets more and more tense in its efforts to speed up. Thus long swinging strides at the walk are vital natural assets to a driving horse.

At the trot, too, long strides are important so that driving horses can make the time in the trot sections of the competition. In the dressage test as well the judges like to see them 'point their toe' (swing their front legs well forward) and show an ability easily to extend their stride. Collection is not as important as in ridden dressage, and a long swinging action at the trot is sought rather than the more rounded springy action which does not cover so much ground and needs a rider in the saddle to generate the power to produce extensions.

Driving has an added requirement to most equestrian sports, which is that the horses must work as a team: their action in particular, their height, size, type and if possible colour should be similar. To create a team, five horses have to be found which look good and move well together. A spare is needed in case of injury, illness, or simply to change the horses around to give variety to their work.

CHANGES THROUGH TRAINING

Probably the most important change made to a driving horse through training is in its character. The horses need to develop complete trust in their Whip and total obedience to him in every situation. Driving can be a very dangerous sport if a horse panics and tries to bolt rather than listening to his Whip. The training entails a form of brain-washing, so that the horse's natural instinct to flee when frightened is transformed into reliance on the Whip to help it out of trouble. A good carriage horse should lose its instinctive urge to gallop away from trouble and, ideally, stand still instead.

The gaits of the carriage horse are not made gymnastic to the same extent as they are with a dressage horse. The major aim is that the team should move in harmony, that the animals should work together with the same length of stride and the same lift to the strides. This entails minor, and sometimes even major, adjustments being made to each of the horses.

Training is used to develop a greater range to the horses' strides. The longer these can be made the easier it will be for them to complete the marathon sections in the time allowed and the better they can extend in the dressage. The shorter the strides, the easier it will be to tackle tricky

Fig. 57 A fit driving horse which is well muscled up and has a rounded appearance without being fat.

hazards and the higher the marks they will gain for the collected movements in the dressage test.

Fitness is a very important aspect in the training of the driving trials horse. Much of the work is directed towards this end, to develop both its powers of endurance for the long marathon and its strength to pull the carriage up hills. A carriage horse when ready for competitions should look round but not fat, with well-developed muscles in the top of the neck and the hindquarters.

TRAINING

Obedience

The horses must be made absolutely obedient to the voice. Only one person ever uses his voice so that they become familiar with the differentiations in tone used for different orders. A simple pattern of commands is adopted and the same commands with the same tone always used for a particular situation – for example, 'Walk on' when wanted to walk, 'Trrrrot', and so on. Chatter is not advisable when schooling for it can confuse the horses, which must learn to respond to the one voice and to distinguish its commands.

Each horse, too, must understand when it is being spoken to by the Whip. It must know when the Whip calls its name, so that it may be corrected if it is pulling too hard,

Peter Munt training a young horse at home. Before the horse is driven in a carriage, it is first driven in long-reins and then pulling a log in order to get it accustomed to the noise and feel of a slight weight behind.

A vital factor in training is to get the horses to work together. This pair of wheelers is beautifully synchronized, with strides of the same length and height.

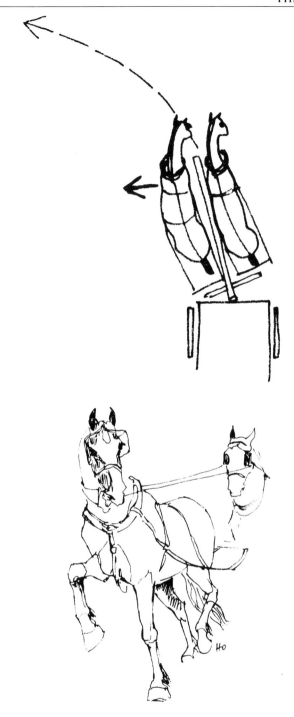

not working hard enough, or playing around. Sometimes a Whip will train a horse to recognize its name with the help of little stones. When he requires something of one of the horses, or to stop it misbehaving, he will throw a few stones on to its hindquarters, speak the horse's name and issue the command. With repetition the horse will learn to respond.

Obedience is instilled from an early age. The horses are carefully handled in the stables and discipline is applied at all times. Especially in the early days of training, when harnessed up to the carriage they are made to stand still for half an hour or more and not allowed to move at all. Nobody holds their heads but people walk around them, and there is always somebody ready to step in if a horse starts to move. This procedure is made into a routine, for any routine promotes relaxation. Having to stand still in this way each time helps to remove tension created by the association that every time they are harnessed to a carriage they are due for action.

Confidence is essential when establishing obedience, and the horses must build up trust in their Whip. Thus in the schooling every precaution is taken to avoid problems and the horses are never asked to do anything beyond their capabilities. Courage is most important in the two leaders for the two wheelers merely follow. They are selected for their boldness, and must obey the Whip when he asks them to go through an apparently terrifying obstacle.

Another means of developing obedience is through riding, for the mounted person has the extra aids of seat and legs, and therefore has more control than the Whip. The voice is still the major aid used, although if it is not achieving the required result it can be reinforced by legs and sticks. If the voice is used at the same time as these more usual and obvious aids from a rider, its use alone will come to be sufficient in the long run.

The horses are usually ridden in pairs, with one rider on each horse. This form of riding is used to practise negotiating difficult and frightening hazards, to develop the movement – the extensions and collection – to get the horses bending, and to prevent that all too common habit of driving horses of bending towards the outside rather than towards the inside of a corner or circle. This particular fault makes it difficult to maintain rhythm and balance but is hard to prevent or cure without using a rider's legs.

Familiarization

Much of the training is aimed at familiarizing the horses with every possible situation that might be met in competition. The essential factor is that the horses remain calm and

Fig. 58 'Falling in' is one of the commonest faults in driving – the horse, lacking the control of a rider's legs and seat over its hindquarters, bends to the outside of a circle. This is the way a horse naturally turns because it is the easiest way for it to keep a balance. It is not, however, the most efficient way of turning as the horse tends to stiffen and finds it difficult to engage the hindquarters under the body.

Fig. 59 Horses often get a leg over a trace in driving. This understandably tends to frighten the horse, and unless it has *confidence in the Whip and accepts his control it may try to run off.*

obedient throughout and to have experienced previously whatever they may face at an event helps considerably towards this end. Comprehensive preparation is very important if the horses are to develop and maintain that vital confidence in the Whip.

Common accidents, such as traces and poles getting broken and legs going over traces, are recreated. Every possible hazard that might be met in a marathon section is practised. Water is driven through (the horses first having been introduced to it when ridden), frightening looking obstacles and tight bends through trees and the like are negotiated. All possible goings are worked on, the horses being driven through mud, along the roads, up hills and even being taken to the seaside to practise on the sand. It is vital that they feel at home on any type of ground that they might have to face.

Another important area for familiarization is the dressage test, but this must not be practised so much that the horses begin to anticipate the movements. The test is best carried out only three or four times in its entirety, and after this pieces may be picked out or even sections done backwards.

With dressage practise is helpful to the Whip as well as the horses. It is he who has to guide and ask the horses for action at particular points, so it is important that he is attuned to their way of going.

The horses need also to be familiarized with the white boards that surround the arena, as well as the white or sawdust centre line. If they shy away because they are not used to these, they will lose many marks.

Way of going

Peter Munt likes his team to be energetic movers – to be keen to go so that he does not have to push them. It is easier to manage and guide a team which pulls than one which needs pushing. Steering is always easier when the horses are moving forward happily.

Their necks should arch and their faces become more vertical with training (similar to being 'on the bit' in dressage); in this position they usually feel lighter in the hands, but still have that forward feeling. This momentum can be encouraged by giving them interesting work and feeding them very well.

Achieving the right amount of forward pull takes experience and an understanding of horses. The Whip must be familiar with the feel of each horse through the reins, so that he knows how much he can pull a horse before it takes charge and starts to pull him. As the horse is much stronger than a man this can be a dangerous situation! Balancing the need for forward momentum against that of maintaining control is one of the chief arts of driving.

The obstacle phase, the final part of the combined driving when competitors must drive their carriages between the cones. Any knockdowns are penalized, as is a round not completed within the time allowed.

Peter and Anne Munt on the box seat, upholding the tradition in carriage driving of being immaculately turned out.

Right: The Dutch champion Tjeerd Velstra during the dressage phase of combined driving at the Royal Windsor Horse Show. The horses are trotting down the centre line and are remaining calm and straight.

Working as a team

The horses

The horses must learn to work as a team. They are best kept together, stabled in stalls alongside one another. (In stalls horses are tied up, and have enough room to lie down but not to turn round.)

Although they are harnessed in pairs – leaders in front and wheelers behind, next to the carriage – it is important that they work as a team, not as two pairs. Yet there are differences in nature which lead to their suitability for a particular position. The leaders are chosen because they are bold, and are usually smaller and lighter. They are the ones that the Whip steers; the wheelers simply follow.

During training the horses' positions are changed daily, the nearside to offside and wheeler to leader. In this way they do not get too set in their ways, and the Whip can discover which is the best place for each horse on the big occasions. Also if there is an accident the substitute can be driven in any position. One some occasions a leader may start to get nervous or naughty; if he is then transferred to the rear position he is more under control and also in a better position for gaining confidence.

To go well together as a team the horses must take approximately the same length strides. This means that the natural stride of some horses will have to be lengthened and that of others shortened. Much of the training for this is done by riding rather than driving the horses, for with the aid of the seat and legs the rider is more able than the Whip to adjust the length of the horses' strides.

The men

The Whip is the key figure, but to run a driving team assistance is needed. The Whip is only as good as his grooms because of the safety aspect. It is dangerous for the Whip to relinquish control by getting down from the carriage while his horses are harnessed or even to let go of the reins. He cannot on his own deal with all the frequent problems of driving: if a horse puts a leg over a trace, one groom can go to the leaders' heads and steady them while the second gets the trace back in its correct position.

A great deal of assistance is needed too in the general care of the horses and equipment. The five horses have to be kept in top condition, for apart from their well-being, few marks are earned in the Presentation section unless they are gleaming with health, spotlessly clean and immaculately plaited. Generally this is the work of one groom. The other is kept busy looking after the equipment, the vehicles and the harness, which again must be very clean and in excellent condition.

TIME SCHEDULE

The first six weeks of training a horse which has not pulled a carriage are spent teaching it to be driven as a single. Harness is worn from the beginning. The horse is long-reined and at first nothing is pulled behind it, then a log is used which makes a good loud noise on the roads. Then the horse is driven between long shafts, but with no carriage, and when relaxed and answering to the voice it may be driven as a single in a carriage.

After about six weeks the horse may be tried as one of a pair, first in long reins and then with the carriage and another more experienced horse beside it. As soon as it is relaxed when driven as one of a pair it can join a team. The untrained horse always starts in the wheeler position, and usually spends about one month there. After this the position may be changed as already described.

The training continues, with the horses being taught obedience, familiarization, the ability to operate as team members and a good manner of going. Within about three months a competition may be tried; the horses might lack the experience to win but the shows will act as a useful training ground. Driving horses mature with competitions, and acquire a new lease of life after training on their own.

From spring until mid-summer Peter competes once a fortnight. Each competition improves the horses so long as they are handled so as not to destroy that vital confidence. By August they should be ready for an international competition. With good fortune and skill, therefore, a driving horse of natural talent is working at its peak just eight months after starting training – which is very little compared to the four to five years necessary for training a dressage horse.

Those eight months are demanding. There are no rests except on the day following a competition. Because driving trials are so competitive, high standards must be achieved, and every day is needed for training. Yet with the varied work, Peter's horses do not get bored or tired by the strain of two or more hours schooling each day at home plus fortnightly competitions.

FEEDING

Another reason why the horses do not get bored is that they are so well fed they are always eager to go. They receive huge rations of oats – 18-20 lb (8-9 kg) a day during the season – and some nuts. They also get regular rations of boiled barley and linseed, to keep them round with sleek coats.

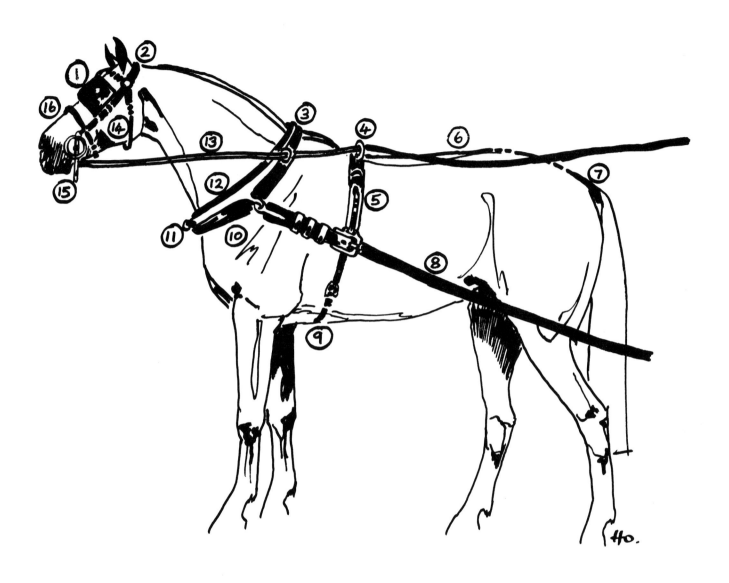

Fig. 60 A horse in harness.

1 Winker	5 Back band	9 Girth	13 Rein
2 Headpiece	6 Back strap	10 Collar	14 Throatlash
3 Top hame strap	7 Crupper	11 Hame chain	15 Liverpool bit
4 Terret	8 Trace	12 Hames	16 Noseband

An obstacle viewed from the box seat of one of the world's foremost Whips, George Bowman.

The water is one of the most spectacular obstacles in the marathon phase. It is hard to pull the carriage through the water and the horses, the leaders in particular, must have great confidence to step off dry land into an unknown depth.

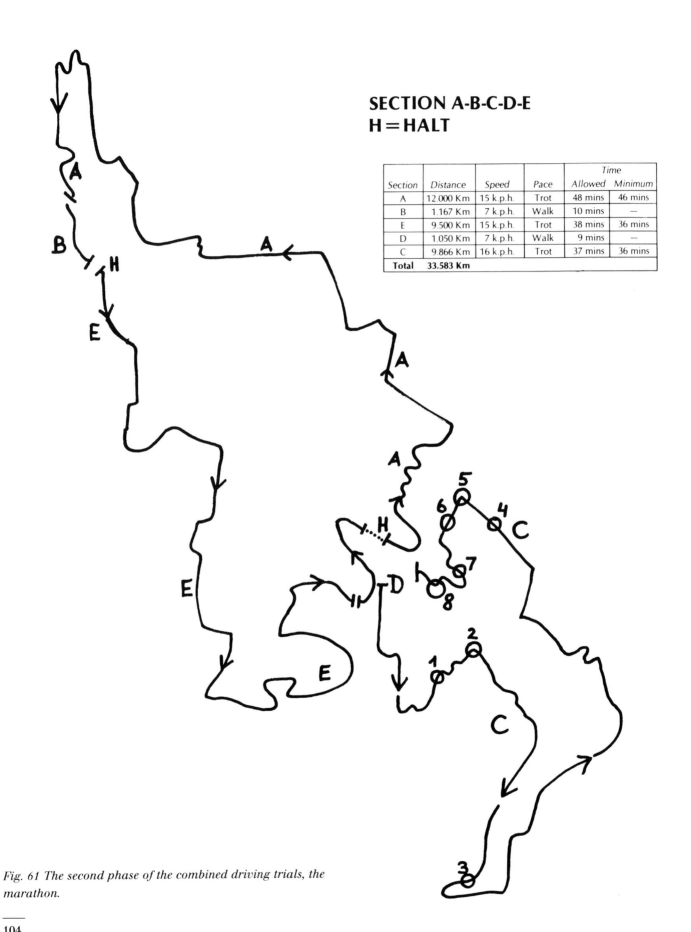

SECTION A-B-C-D-E
H = HALT

Section	Distance	Speed	Pace	Time Allowed	Time Minimum
A	12.000 Km	15 k.p.h.	Trot	48 mins	46 mins
B	1.167 Km	7 k.p.h.	Walk	10 mins	—
E	9.500 Km	15 k.p.h.	Trot	38 mins	36 mins
D	1.050 Km	7 k.p.h.	Walk	9 mins	—
C	9.866 Km	16 k.p.h.	Trot	37 mins	36 mins
Total	**33.583 Km**				

Fig. 61 The second phase of the combined driving trials, the marathon.

FACILITIES

Although it may not be used very often, a piece of flat ground on which a 100×40 metre dressage arena can be erected is necessary. Unlike dressage training, this is used more for familiarization than for improving the horse's way of going.

Most of the schooling time is spent out on the grass and sand tracks and tarmac roads, getting the horses fit as well as used to working in the carriage. It helps if considerable distances of these are available so that the long hours of work can be varied. Hills are useful too in getting the horses into condition and developing their muscles.

As already mentioned, driving horses need the opportunity to practise hazards, and many of these can be found naturally in forests and copses. Others can be made from barrels, posts, boxes and so on. The one essential practice hazard is water, for this is very frightening to the inexperienced horse. To help build up confidence a smooth entry, a firm bottom and shallow water are the important factors.

EQUIPMENT

In driving trials – unlike other equestrian sports – the horse is one of the least expensive items of equipment. Two sets of harness are required for competition work: one smart one for presentation, one strong one for the cross-country, and in addition an old set is needed for breaking in.

The serious competitor must have two carriages. The cross-country carriage is best made of iron which stands up to the rigours of these demanding courses better than wood or other materials. This must weigh the regulation amount of 600 kilos. The weights can be built into the carriage so that they are spread over the four wheels and make it a better balanced carriage. The latest development in cross-country carriage building is a front seat which turns with a pole rather than with the rest of the carriage (like an articulated lorry). Thus the Whip is always with his horses, and this gives a better turning point and the ability to turn tighter through the hazards. It is also a rule that specified spares have to be carried.

The presentation carriage must be in first-class condition; competitors use both modern and authentic old carriages. When they wish to be very smart they use neck collars, black patent leather harness and brass fittings. The emphasis in the presentation section is on an immaculate turnout rather than strength and practicability. Again spares must be carried.

The turnout of the Whip and his grooms is important too. The grooms can be in hunting kit or liveries, but in either case it must be matching, gleaming and well fitted.

A Whip should always carry a whip. The cross-country whip is similar to a lunging whip with a 12 foot ($3\frac{1}{2}$ m) lash so that it is long enough to reach the leaders. During dressage and presentation the traditional holly whip is carried, which is shorter.

THE WHIP

Driving a trained single horse or pony in harness is a possibility for practically any sensible person. Driving four horses is a different matter. It is a difficult task even to drive them in a straight line, let alone guide them through the intricate hazards of competition. For this it is necessary not only to be a skilled Whip but also to build up the essential trust of the horses.

Experience is essential in addition to natural ability, and most of the top coachmen have spent a large part of their lives and a great deal of each day driving horses.

The ability to remain calm in frightening situations such as horses bolting, and the boldness to tackle obstacles with rhythm and positive clear-thinking are both needed. Most good Whips have a history of courageous activities – George Bowman was a bronco rider, the Duke of Edinburgh a polo player and Peter Munt a stunt man.

Judgement is also an important attribute. The horses have to be guided through very narrow twisting routes, and it is vital to know when a direct course can be taken or when a loop is necessary.

Since the hands are the sole physical means of communication with the horses, a good coachman needs hands which can feel what his horses are about to do. He must be able to sense how much contact to take before the horses start to pull against him; control is through give and take, not force.

All these qualities are used to make the most of the horse's natural ability when training. In competitions timing is needed in addition, for sections have to be completed in specified times. The Whip needs to know the gaits of the horses so that he can judge the speed and so complete the sections at a rhythmical, effort-saving pace, rather than changing from fast to slow and vice versa.

This vital attribute for competitive success is however of little value if the horses lack the natural scope to their gaits. As Peter Munt has emphasized, a good natural fast walk is needed to make a horse worth training for top competitions and enable a Whip to exercise his feel for timing.

Polo

Julian Hipwood

INTRODUCTION

Polo is the oldest equestrian sport considered in this book. It is described in a Persian manuscript dated 600 BC, which means that it has been played for more than 2500 years. Today most equestrian-minded countries have polo grounds where the game is practised but only a few nations (Argentina, the USA, New Zealand, Australia, Spain and Britain) can field teams of high goal players.

High goal players are those with high handicaps. The handicaps range from −2 to +10: a beginner will receive −2, and the best in the world +10. These handicaps, as in golf, are used to make a match more competitive. Thus a team whose four members' handicaps add up to, say, 24 goals (this would be a high goal team) would be awarded 0 goals at the start of the match, but the opposing team whose handicaps added up to only 22 goals would be credited with the difference of 2 goals at the start of a six chukker match. If there are fewer chukkers to the match, the difference between the two totals, in this case two, is multiplied by the number of chukkers (usually four) and divided by six, which is the number of chukkers on which the handicaps are based.

Each chukker lasts for seven minutes, and the players change their ponies between chukkers, because the game is so fast and demanding that the ponies could not be expected to work for longer.

Polo is a very fast game, for with a ground which can be as large as 270 × 180 metres the ponies reach nearly 30

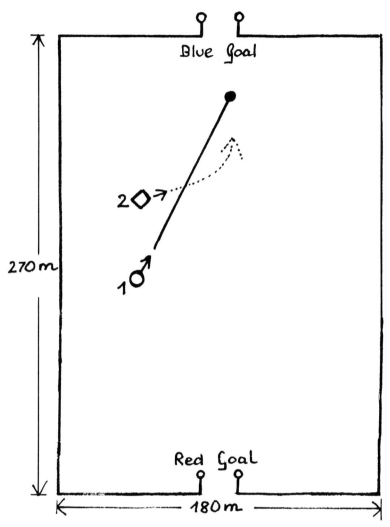

Fig. 62 The polo field. The diagram shows two players: 1 is following the line of the ball (the black dot) and has the right of way over all others. Player no. 2 as he follows the dotted line will cross the line of the ball and will be penalized.

mph (48 kph). With such speed and the possibility of players coming from a variety of directions towards the ball there is a danger of serious collisions. Rules are therefore needed to ensure reasonable safety for ponies and riders in this potentially hazardous game. The main necessity is to clarify who has the right of way, and this is awarded to whichever player is following the line of the ball. Any opponent crossing the line or path of the player who has acquired the right of way is penalized. There are two mounted umpires to enforce this rule, obviously a difficult task since the game is so fast and the line of the ball changes frequently. In case of a dispute the third rule keeper, the referee, who is seated on the edge of the field, adjudicates.

This right of way is the only major rule – players can hook their opponents' sticks, and even push opponents off the line of the ball by bumping their horse (riding-off). It is a rough, exhilarating sport, demanding strength, courage and talent from both horse and rider. Polo is one equestrian sport in which girls rarely excel, for the sympathetic relationship with the horse which takes them so far in show jumping, eventing and dressage is of little value in polo. A good eye for the ball, ruthless determination to get to the ball, and the strength to manoeuvre the horse and ward off opponents are much more important. Horsemanship plays an important part in the training of a polo pony, but very little in the game itself.

One confusing point to the layman is that the animals used are called ponies, yet they are in fact horses standing between 14.3 and 15.3 hands high. Originally they were smaller and true ponies, but as the game speeded up so did the demand for faster, larger beasts, which today are still called polo ponies.

NATURAL TALENTS
The shape

Polo is a demanding exercise for the horse, both physically and mentally. A young horse when first ridden is unbalanced and awkward in its movements and only after good training will it be able to make the sudden transitions in pace and direction which the game demands. Some horses do show a natural aptitude for polo (unfortunately they are few and far between), and for these the training will be quicker and their talents obvious when ridden by even a moderately good player.

Julian keeps the following points in mind when looking for a suitable type of animal to train for polo (while bearing in mind that there are exceptions to every rule, and that

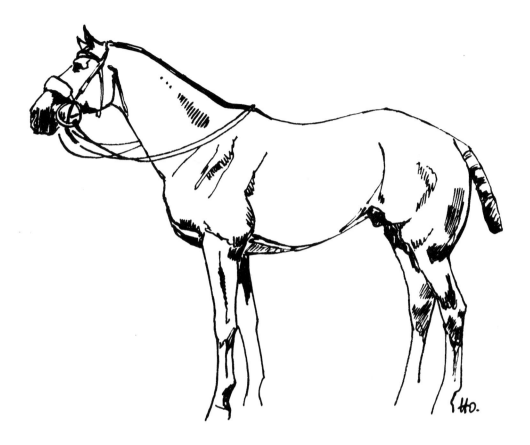

Fig. 63 A polo pony when fit, shown with a gag bit and a bandaged tail. Its legs will need bandages or boots before it is asked to play. It should be a good deal leaner than the unfit version (Fig. 65).

some very unlikely looking horses have, in the past, proved to be brilliant polo ponies). A short-backed horse with well-sprung ribs can usually turn and stop more quickly. A wide chest and hindquarters are useful too, as a narrow weedy type will not be of much use in the case of a hard bump. A generous shoulder with plenty of depth is important, again for those heavy bumps. A good natural head carriage is an advantage, for if the horse is overbent stopping can become a problem and if it sticks its nose out and resists the hand, both stopping and turning will be difficult. Good withers help to keep the saddle in the correct position: poor withers on a polo pony can be very dangerous, because of the amount of movement the rider must make in the saddle. The neck should be neither too long nor too short, and a thick heavy neck is most undesirable. Legs should not be too long, with a good amount of bone. Pasterns may generally be slightly straighter than is usually acceptable in horses required for other activities, since their opposite, long sloping pasterns, put too much strain on the tendons which are subjected to great wear and tear in polo. Overall the horse should have a harmonious conformation, and this will help it to be naturally balanced in its movement.

Beware of taking a thoroughbred which has been racing, because its temperament must be suspect. A year or so of galloping flat out on a racecourse is not conducive to stopping and turning in a matter of yards. There are exceptions, however, and some brilliant polo ponies playing in England and America today began their lives on the racecourse. But ex-racehorses must be selected with great care, and allowance should be made for a longer training period. Another danger with pure-bred thoroughbreds is that they tend to be a little light of bone and are less likely to stand up to the rigours of polo.

The Argentine polo pony is Julian's favourite. The Argentines have developed an animal for polo, which, though not a breed as such, has become a standard type. These ponies are descended from the indigenous horse of

The ball lies ahead of these two players and to their right. The player on the right is 'riding-off' his opponent which entails pushing him away from the ball.

Left: Polo ponies are usually bridled with four reins. The reins are held in the left hand. The top reins are held between the thumb and index finger and can be shortened by being pulled through with the right hand which holds the polo stick. The second pair of reins (the more severe ones) are held between the third and fourth fingers. Direction is controlled by moving the left hand to the left or right (neck-reining). The horse is stopped by initially using the top reins, and if necessary the more severe bottom reins.

Fig. 64 A polo player using neck-reining to turn his mount.

South America, the Criollo, having been crossed over many generations with varying strains of blood horses. The result is a standardized horse which combines the three most important attributes in a polo pony: speed, a docile temperament and physical strength. These are the natural features needed in a polo pony no matter at what type of horse or where in the world you may be looking.

TRAINING

The early training of a young unbroken horse for polo differs little from that given to a horse destined for any other equestrian sport. Life for the young polo pony begins with gentle handling, then lunging (and long-reining if there is time, but this is a precious commodity in the polo business), followed by backing, in the normal manner. The English system of polo training usually requires the use of first a mouthing bit (Fig. 67), followed by a snaffle bit.

Most animals respond to routine teaching, and the horse is no exception. Reward and punishment should be used as necessary. There is no absolute for training a horse for polo, it is merely a question of personal preference – the same end result is required, but the methods of achieving it vary not only from country to country, but from horseman to horseman.

It is important to pay attention to the physical condition of the horse so that it does not become above itself with over-generous feeding, for if this happens the horse will be more difficult to handle. On the other hand if the horse is in poor condition it will not respond to the aids that it is given.

The rider's legs, hands and voice are the most important aids, as with training any horse, but for the polo pony the hand aids are different, since it must learn to stop very quickly and straight, with pressure from one hand only. Where polo pony training varies so dramatically from normal schooling is that a polo pony must be taught to neck-rein – that is, it must turn to left or right in response to pressure of the rein on the opposite side of the neck. The whip is also a necessary aid which, although seldom used, is not forgotten by the horse and will tend to make it behave in a more amenable manner.

The first few months of training will have nothing to do with polo; the young horse must learn to walk and trot in a collected manner, and to canter on the correct leg while maintaining as good a balance as possible. Balance is never perfect in the beginning, but time and muscular development soon lead to improvement.

It is important for the young horse to be worked in an enclosed area; a rectangular school with solid walls is ideal, and certainly a fence of some sort is necessary to work against when teaching the horse to stop and turn.

The mouth of the young polo pony is like any other horse's at this early stage, but gradually it must be made more sensitive. This is achieved by stopping and reining back several times on every circuit, at a walk and then at a trot. When the horse will do this willingly and without getting upset, it should be taught to turn by neck-reining. The horse is walked towards the wall or fence of the school, and when about 3½-4½ metres away is stopped and turned 180° into the corner, all the time remaining correctly bent and with the hocks well under the body. This work may progress so that the turns are then done from the trot and finally the canter, but always by neck-reining.

Up to this stage the snaffle is the bit most regularly used on the young horse. Many horses do go better in a pelham, however (Fig. 68), and it is for the trainer to determine what suits his horse best.

Changing legs is usually one of the last movements to be taught before the horse has its first glimpse of a polo stick. This is taught by work on figures of eight. To begin with the horse is brought back from a canter to a trot for a few strides in the middle of the figure and then asked to strike off into the canter on the other leg. When the horse understands this, it can be asked for a flying change, that is changing the leading legs in the canter during the moment of suspension. All that matters is for the leads to be

Fig. 65 A good type of polo pony: the shape is harmonious and balanced. Note the pasterns, which are much straighter than the ideal in other sports.

Julian Hipwood in a training session demonstrates how to turn his horse very quickly through neck-reining, and adjusting his weight – first backwards to reduce the horse's speed and engage the hind legs under the body, then towards the direction of the turn to help the horse move that way. (Note: although hats are only compulsory during games it is recommended that riders wear them even during training.)

Left: Hooking of sticks. This is another permissible means of preventing an opponent from hitting the ball.

Right: This shot is called an offside back-hander. Julian Hipwood is hitting the ball in the opposite direction to that in which he and his pony are moving.

changed; unlike dresssage, the quality of the movement is unimportant. Therefore it does not matter whether the horse throws its head, swings its hindquarters or loses its rhythm – training for polo is not artistic, it is purely practical.

Many moves in polo rely on the horse being able to change direction only slightly. Making 180° turns is not the only requirement: the horse must be trained to be agile and able to adjust its feet quickly and nimbly during only slight changes of direction.

When the young horse is being worked in the school or just hacked outside during winter, it is helpful for the rider to carry a polo stick. It should be swung gently around the horse, in all directions but without any sudden movements. As soon as the pony realizes that the stick will cause no harm it should remain relaxed whenever the stick is used.

The appearance of the ball is another matter, and even horses with apparent natural talent for polo will continue to shy off the ball for quite some time. Perhaps it is the sound of the ball being hit, or the sight of it bouncing around that makes a horse wary. Even experienced horses with several seasons of polo behind them will often watch the ball in their first few chukkers of a new season. Time and patience will correct this.

It is also important for the young horse to become accustomed to the proximity of other horses on the polo field, especially when they are moving fast. Before trying any chukkers, it is advisable to play some 'stick and ball' – a few players practising hitting the ball but without trying to score goals. The young horse can be ridden close to the others so that it gets used to being touched by the other horses while the ball is being hit off it. Riding-off is an important feature of the game: two opposing players ride alongside and deliberately bump each other, trying to push the other out of the way in order to get enough room to strike the ball. A horse which will not go in for a ride-off will be useless as a polo pony. Another potentially frightening part of the game is approaching other horses from head on at a fast pace, so the horse must get used to this when practising stick and ball.

The next stage is the practice chukker, when eight riders get together to play as two teams, but with training as the sole object. In these the young horse should never be pushed so much that it becomes unruly or wild; it is very exciting to be galloping surrounded by seven other horses, and even more so for a horse from the racetrack which is used to racing against other horses. All ponies must be taken very carefully at this stage. The speed at which the young horse is played should only gradually be increased in practice chukkers until the horse is steady enough to be taken into match games. Obviously winning is important in a match, and no matter how carefully the player intends to take his young horse, such intentions can easily be forgotten in the heat of the moment. But a player who is tempted to rush a young horse may find that all the hard work of the past months is irreparably damaged. The first matches may be less than a year from when the horse's training started, so in this initial season and even the following one, the games are still used as a means of training.

TIME SCHEDULE

The weather in Britain is a problem for those embarking on training their own polo ponies. The ideal time to start working on the young horse is in September, but with the advent of winter, conditions become difficult unless an indoor school or artificial arena is available. By April, when most clubs start chukkers again, the young horse should have become accustomed to the polo stick and the ball, and to their use in the company of other horses. He should be able to start playing but in this first season he will only be learning as training cannot reasonably be completed in less than one and a half to two years.

ARGENTINIAN METHODS

The Argentines are, quite rightly, considered to be the world's best polo players, and on the whole their horses are also the best. Their methods of training polo ponies are quite different from the other main polo playing countries (Britain, the United States, New Zealand, Australia, Spain), and to some might appear cruel. Their attitude towards the breaking of a horse is simply to have the matter dealt with as quickly as possible. They aim totally to dominate the will of the animal by breaking its spirit, in contrast to the British method in which man and horse meet half way. There is an abundance of horses in Argentina, and it is therefore impossible for an outsider to gauge the success and failure rate of the Argentine methods of polo pony training.

The breaking of a horse is treated as fun by the gauchos, the Argentinian cowboys. A horse is tied very tightly with a headcollar and rope to a post in a field. It is then blindfolded and a saddle is put on its back, whereupon it is mounted by a gaucho. The horse is then turned loose, and with the blindfold removed gallops off, leaping and kicking. The horse is obviously terrified, but it is made to keep galloping and bucking until it has no fight left and no longer has the energy to object to the rider on its back.

Instead of a conventional bit, a rawhide strap is used in

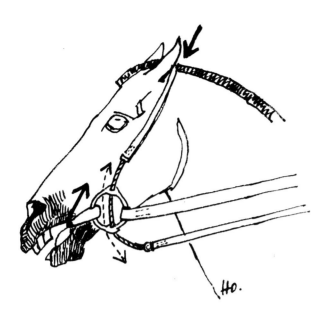

Fig. 66 A gag. When the rider uses the top rein it acts merely as a snaffle, but when the bottom rein is used the bit is pulled higher into the horse's mouth and pressure is applied to the poll – both of which help to make the horse stop.

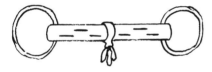

Fig. 67 A mouthing bit which is used on the young horse because it is gentle in its action. The keys in the centre encourage the horse to champ at the bit and develop that white foam which is the sign of a good mouth.

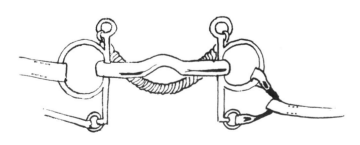

Fig. 68 A short-shanked pelham with a port (a kink in the centre of the bit). This may be used with two reins (left), in which case the effect of the top rein is relatively gentle, but the bottom rein will bring into use the curb chain which tightens against the horse's chin. On the right rounders are used with one rein, when the effect is neither so mild as use of the top rein alone nor as severe as the bottom rein.

the mouth to teach the horse to stop. The strap is tied tightly around the lower jaw (with the tongue above it) and joined to a small metal ring, to which the reins are attached. The rider teaches the horse to stop by using all his body weight to apply sudden pulls on the reins. This is an infinitely faster training method than the conventional one, and the horse's tongue is never actually touched. The strap is used for a few months, during which time the horse learns astonishingly quickly to anticipate the violent tug on the reins, and stops extremely quickly. Following this initial stage the first bit to be put in the horse's mouth is usually a short-shanked pelham, with a high port (see Fig. 68). This will allow the horse freedom for its tongue while preventing it from curling it over the top of the bit, which it may try to do having been used to the leather strap tied below the tongue. (A horse's tongue must remain under the bit, for it is the pressure on the tongue which gives the rider control. Horses which evade this control by putting their tongue over the bit are often runaways.) After more work with the pelham some horses will be put into a gag (Fig. 66) to raise the head. Most Argentinian ponies will have a sensitive mouth by this stage but are usually behind the bit, that is with the head tucked in close to the chest.

Having mastered the art of stopping very quickly, the Argentinian pony is then taught to turn and neck-rein. It is turned against a fence in much the same way as its counterpart in England, but with the aid of a *rebenke*, a short leather-covered stick with a loose leather flap 25-30 cm long on the end. The rebenke is flapped against the side of the horse's neck and head, and its natural inclination is to turn away as quickly as it can from the rebenke. In a very short time it will turn through 180° without any trouble.

The horse is now ready for stick and ball, but most gauchos simply put the horse into slow chukkers on the *estancia*, the Argentinian ranch. Up to this stage the young horse is usually only ridden by a gaucho, but if it shows itself to be of some worth in the practice chukkers the Argentine polo player will try it out. The gauchos specializing in the training of polo ponies are called *domodors*, or rough-riders, and not surprisingly these are very important men on the farm of a polo player; to lose a good domodor can seriously affect the standard of a high goal player's string of ponies.

Only many years of experience, the riding of hundreds of different horses, the watching of polo at all levels and in many different countries, can possibly give an insight into the best methods of training polo ponies. Julian has experienced all this, and feels that a combination of the different schools of thought is in the end most successful.

Racing

Michael Stoute

INTRODUCTION

Flat racing is a major international industry. Billions of pounds change hands each year in betting, and millions more in the attempt to find a top racehorse, or a stallion to produce the racehorses. Yet a sporting atmosphere still prevails, probably because the unpredictable nature of racing means that nobody is ever certain of a profit. In this hazardous sport top jockeys may hurt themselves, top trainers may find their star horses devastated by viruses, top owners may waste millions on their purchases (for money does not buy success: many great winners are cheap, many valuable purchases are useless), and top stud owners may see their most expensive stallions become worthless through infertility or failing to reproduce their own virtues in their offspring. It is all a big gamble, and that is what makes racing so exciting – so heartbreaking and expensive when it goes wrong, so exhilarating and remunerative when it comes right.

Racing too covers a very wide spectrum, from the country tracks with perhaps an annual meeting and very little prize money for the amateur participants, to the multi-million pound racecourses in the United States, France, Britain, Australia and Hong Kong where races worth tens of thousands of pounds are held.

The major races among leading nations are called the classics, in which the horses run at level weights. In Britain, home of the breed of racehorses (thoroughbred) and serious racing, these are for three-year-olds. They are the one mile 2,000 Guineas for colts and 1,000 Guineas for fillies, the 1½ mile Derby for colts and Oaks for fillies, and the 1¾ mile St Leger, open to both sexes. The ultimate aim is to win all three, thus earning the Triple Crown.

The American classics are run over a smaller range of distances and also during a shorter period – two months as opposed to Europe's five-month span. The races are the 10 furlong Kentucky Derby, the 9½ furlong Preakness, and the 12 furlong Belmont, with the equivalents for fillies being over 8, 9 and 10 furlongs. (A furlong is one-eighth of a mile, or 200 metres.)

In France there are six classic races, the 8 furlong Poule d'Essai des Poulains and Poule d'Essai des Pouliches, the 12 furlong Prix du Jockey Club, the 15½ furlong Grand Prix de Paris, the 10½ furlong Prix de Diane and the 15½ furlong Prix Royal Oak. The greatest French race, however, is the 12 furlong Prix de l'Arc de Triomphe, but this is not a classic for it is open to older horses as well as to three-year-olds, the age determining the weights.

In Australia the classics are even less important. There the great race is the 16 furlong Melbourne Cup, a handicap in which weights are allotted with the aim of equalizing the horses' abilities – thus the horse which in the opinion of the handicapper is the best will carry the most weight. Throughout the racing world the handicap is by far the most common type of race.

The distances of flat races vary from 5 furlongs to about 20 furlongs. No horse will excel at all distances, and one of the skills of training is to ascertain the best distance for each horse. Pedigree is a good indicator, for a horse rarely runs a great deal further or faster than its parents. Shape is another: the typical sprinter, over 5-7 furlongs, is relatively compact, with powerful hindquarters to help it accelerate over the short distance, whereas the typical stayer, over 12 furlongs plus, is lean and rangy. Each horse has its range of two to three furlongs over which it will be at its best; over a shorter distance it will be too slow, over a longer distance it will 'blow up'.

Age also plays a part in the horse's optimum distance. As a horse gets older it can run further, so that stayers are at their best from four years old onwards while sprinters are more precocious and are usually retired by that age. Two-year-olds are not raced over more than 8 furlongs, and most start their racetrack career over 5 or 6 furlongs.

The racehorse trainer's job is to recognize and buy horses with natural ability, and then to develop through training the disposition which will enable them to make use of this ability, together with the necessary physical fitness. He must ascertain the distance over which the horse's ability is greatest, the type of going – heavy, firm, grass, dirt – which it prefers, and the standard of race in which it has a chance of winning.

NATURAL TALENTS

The racehorse trainer has a great deal more practice in selecting horses than trainers in other equestrian spheres. A leading trainer like Michael Stoute is involved in the buying of about twenty horses a year. His skills of selection are crucial, for not only has he, like all trainers, his personal reputation at stake but also huge sums of other people's money – every year he has orders to buy yearlings for hundreds of thousands of pounds. This does not, however, stop him from also buying cheap ones.

The money that Michael has to spend on a horse determines how good a pedigree he can select. He looks for similar points in shape, action and outlook in every horse he chooses to train, but when he has big money to play with he can go for blue-blooded material. In this case, he will do a lot of research from the sales catalogue, which states the pedigree of all horses in the sale. The ancestors of the potential purchase must be carefully checked to ascertain their class both on the racecourse and as parents, and to see that the proportions of sprinting, classic and staying blood are in harmony and likely to produce the required horse.

Fig. 69 A racehorse showing a pleasing free walk.

Fig. 70 'Piggy' ears such as these usually indicate a mean character. The tendon is bowed – curved outwards rather than straight – which shows that it has been strained.

A good pedigree may give a horse value as a stud animal, particularly in the case of fillies, despite a disappointing performance record, but it is the latter which is the vital factor. To prove themselves on the racecourse horses must stay sound. Tremendous strain is placed on the forelegs, and the tendons are particularly at risk at the end of the race when the horse is tired. Strained tendons and knee problems are causes of ending or interrupting a horse's short racing career, so the foreleg is the first place most trainers' eyes travel to when considering soundness.

Action

Size is a less important factor than athleticism in a racehorse. The animal must use itself when moving, pushing itself from behind and using its hindlegs, which should be placed well under the body. The shoulder too should swing freely. None of the movements, however, should put strain on any particular part of the body. It is this athleticism which is the key factor in a racehorse. It will show in the swing of the walk, the spring to the trot – but at the sales, where most flat horses are bought, the canter cannot be tested. It is an advantage if the horse can be seen free in the fields for although the yearling will not have developed the gallop, if it moves well at the canter it is more likely to turn out fast.

Temperament

The other vital factor – the animal's character – cannot be tested either. Horses with piggy ears (small and slightly curved) can be avoided, horses with good bold eyes can be given a chance, but these are only hazy indications of a future attitude.

A 'star' has to have a competitive nature and eagerness to battle when in a tight finish with other horses, so Michael favours the youngsters showing some exuberance. Yet a racehorse also has to be able to relax, to be able to 'switch off'. If it is tense and jumpy all the time it uses up energy and will not be able to make the most of itself in a race. This applies particularly in Britain, where races are run tactically rather than flat out from start to finish. Horses gallop at a slower speed in the first part of the race and only accelerate into top gear towards the end.

The difficulty of selecting a star performer is reflected by the records. Some of the very expensive yearlings have had relatively poor performances, and some of the inexpensive yearlings have beaten their more blue-blooded and valuable rivals.

CHANGES THROUGH TRAINING

Racing is the most natural of the major equestrian sports. The horse has to be taught very little other than to accept the weight of the rider and a certain amount of control by him. The major role of the trainer is to make it easy to use the horse's ability, so although a particularly good trainer will help a good horse to gallop marginally faster, the difference in performance extracted by good and bad trainers is not so great as in other sports. The excellence of a racehorse trainer is judged in terms of the horses he selects, how sound he can keep them, how fit he can get and maintain them, and how skilfully he chooses the appropriate race for each horse (known as placing).

The most important change which Michael likes to see in his horses is that they learn to relax, even under tension-creating circumstances. A great deal of the training, in and out of his yard, is geared to making this change. A few horses of course are naturally relaxed, but this is rare among thoroughbreds in general and even rarer among those which have the ability and competitiveness to win big races.

Physically the horses will change a good deal. When they enter a British yard they are still yearlings, so that some natural growth and a good deal of maturing will occur while they are in training. In the process of reaching peak fitness – the major aim in training – their muscles become more rounded and increase their tone and hardness. The muscles developed are those behind the saddle and in the hindquarters, and this is particularly noticeable as the horses age from two- to three-year-olds.

Michael takes care to ensure that the muscles developed are confined to those used for galloping, since any extras

Flat racing takes place in the summer or in southern countries where the climate is good, consequently having to train under conditions such as these is rare. The horses seen here cantering in the snow are 'jumpers', horses which race over fences. These races are held in wintertime. Jumpers are, however, older horses which do not race until they are nearly four years at a minimum and are therefore usually tougher and able to take such strains.

The auction ring at Keeneland, Lexington, Kentucky.

A trainer's yard, showing one lad carrying saddlery and another a fork for cleaning out the stables.

In flat races the horses start out of stalls to ensure that they all have a fair start. This can be a frightening experience, so young horses have to be familiarized with the stalls at home.

Before the youngsters are ridden they get used to the feel of the saddlery and learn to be guided by reins to the bit. For this purpose long-reins are used in the manner shown here.

Fig. 71 The fit racehorse is much leaner and less muscle-bound than horses in other sports.

are unnecessary and might be actually restrictive. Consequently the work of the horses soon to race is confined in the main to cantering and galloping. Hill work, swimming and other types of exercise may be used early in the conditioning work, but because of the danger of developing other muscles this will be discontinued as the time for racing approaches.

Another result of the fittening process should be a tremendous change in the capacity of the lungs and heart. This of course is not visible but is judged by the amount of blowing a horse does after work. This is one of the trainer's major guides to deciding how close the horse is to peak fitness, and how much and what type of work is needed to get it there without straining its heart and lungs. It is now possible to measure pulse rate by the use of various instruments, but the experienced trainer with the special understanding he has of his horses gauges the heart and lung capacity largely from their manner of blowing after work.

Good trainers try to get to know each individual horse well enough to be able to ascertain how much can be changed. They have to judge the character and potential of the animal – a task made easier if they have had the experience of training the parents, for many factors are inherited.

The problem of course is that the trainer cannot explain to a horse that the grind of getting fit and galloping its heart out is worth while. Unlike human runners the horses do not have the incentive of medals, glory or money to spur them through painful barriers. Horses will snap mentally and stop trying if pushed too hard. The trainer must know just

how far he can push his horses, for he can never force or frighten them into winning races; they have to want to do so.

TRAINING
Relaxation

An important facet of training is to teach the horse to relax. Everything is geared towards this. Any horse that starts to pull to get to the lead when working, to run too free, is kept at the back of a group of well-behaved horses (known as being 'dropped right out'). It is important to catch the young horse in time to prevent it from ever tensing up and attempting to gallop off.

After the work the pupils must again be able to relax. They should walk quietly home and if one starts to jog it is 'buried' in the centre of the string of racehorses where, surrounded by relaxed horses, it will soon learn to calm down. For the last part of the walk home Michael likes the lads to get off, loosen the girths and lead their horses.

In the stable the same aim of relaxation is pursued. All activities are kept to a regular routine – feeds, grooming, exercise are always given at the same time. The attitude of the boys towards the horses is carefully monitored, and the staff are kept happy so that the atmosphere in the yard is relaxed.

A horse that has been taught to relax can direct its energy towards winning and not use it up needlessly before the race or in the early stages.

Keenness

At the same time as learning to relax, the horse must be kept mentally keen, which means that it must not be asked more than it is capable of giving. This is a major factor when training two-year-olds which after all are merely adolescents. The maturity of each horse has to be assessed so that it is not subject to the rigours of hard training and being prepared for a race unless it is physically ready for the work. Two-year-olds' careers have to be adjusted to their growth – precocious youngsters may run when barely two years old, but big, gangly types may be better kept off the course until they are three. Without such adjustments to individual maturity, good horses may be ruined.

The other way of keeping horses keen and competitive is to vary the place of work. This becomes more important when they are being worked hard and galloping frequently. By then the horses should have learned to relax and are now under the strain of trying to achieve maximum performance, so Michael varies the areas of ground to help keep their interest.

THE TIME SCHEDULE

The careers of the top racehorses are compressed into less than two years. Their competitive work is over before horses destined for other equestrian sports are even broken. As yearlings they enter training in mid-winter, usually race a few times as two-year-olds in the summer and then have to prove themselves in the big races as three-year-olds. The successes are then worth millions of pounds at stud, so they are usually hastily retired. It is too big a risk for the owner to put the proven horse back on the track where it might be damaged or lose its reputation with a poor performance. In the United States however the races for older horses have bigger prize money than in Europe so the risk is more worth while and more horses are raced as four- and five-year-olds. In Europe usually it is only the long distance horses, which are not ready to run until they are older, that enjoy longer careers.

Horses in Europe which are not so successful and therefore not worth so much at stud are either sold to lesser racing countries, such as South America, West Indies or the Middle East where they will be more competitive, or if they are strong enough, start a new career racing over fences.

The first few months

At an age when most young horses are still running free in the fields the racehorse is brought into training. Even the first 18 months could not be described as 'natural', for the potential racehorse will have been fed to the maximum and handled continuously in order to prepare for its early career. The yearlings come to Michael's yard between October and December and then spend a month or more being lunged or in long-reins (see page 132). Part of the long-reining work will include the introduction to starting stalls. For sensitive hyper-fit animals to stand quietly in these minute partitions just before they race flat out would seem contrary to natural behaviour, but with this early training they accept it as part of the work and very few eruptions are seen on the racecourse.

After the work from the ground, the first three or four weeks with the rider up are spent walking and trotting. The aim is to build up the muscles and to get the horses very much fitter so that they can stand up to the more demanding canter work. They then start going out on the gallops and each horse is assessed as to when it can begin cantering. With the owners paying big training bills and the lure of glory and remuneration on the racetrack for two-year-olds, there is a pressure on trainers to prepare the horse for the track as quickly as possible, but this must be balanced against the risk of damaging the horse mentally or physically by taking it too fast.

Learning to gallop

From the New Year onwards the yearlings start cantering. They begin over 2½ furlongs and are gradually asked for longer stretches until they can keep it up over 4 furlongs. The next stage is a second canter, in the same training session but at a steady pace. Next, instead of cantering one behind the other, they start going 'upsides', that is cantering and galloping in a group of two or more. Michael likes his horses to work in a bunch and to keep very close so that they get accustomed to being surrounded by other horses as in a race. Cantering alongside other horses brings out the competitiveness in the youngsters, but at this stage relaxation is the primary aim. Any horses which start to try and pull to the lead are allowed to do so once but not twice, for then they are kept behind the other horses and forced to drop what might develop into the wasteful habit of running too 'free'.

Cantering is always preceded by a walk of at least twenty minutes; in cold weather it may be longer, for it is important that the horses should be warmed up before they begin to gallop. The trotting is gradually reduced as it does not develop the muscles needed for galloping, until those in intense work do no more than trot a few strides so that the trainer can check if they are sound, the trot being the easiest pace at which to detect any lameness.

By the beginning of the year the youngsters are exercising for about one hour and ten minutes. For the three-year-olds and upwards this is gradually increased until when in full work they are out of the stables for an hour and three-quarters. Much of this time will be spent at the walk: the warming up period, the recovery between canters, and the 'unwinder' on the way home.

When getting fit they will have what are known as 'swinging canters', but progress to canters at half speed as the season approaches, and eventually the full speed, galloping work starts. Most horses will have up to two galloping sessions a week but as soon as they start racing there is no regular pattern – it depends on the horse and on the type and dates of the races.

The galloping is done over a great variety of distances. To begin with the horses are worked over short distances but these are gradually lengthened until, as the day of the race approaches, the distance (trip) is shortened in order to sharpen up the horses, the emphasis being shifted to speed rather than staying power.

This work is of course relative to the type of horses, as

A training spin in which the horse is showing tremendous athleticism and length of stride. It is wearing a quarter rug to keep it warm in the delicate area behind the saddle.

Working upsides (two horses together) on a 'dirt' track. Both horses are showing a pronounced moment of suspension.

A string of horses walking back to the stables at the major racing centre of Chantilly in France.

two-year-olds and sprinters never gallop over as long distances as the older horses and stayers, who in their turn are rarely galloped over the shortest distances.

Michael's approach to each galloping session is to begin with the horses 'off the bridle' (not pulling) and just going easily at half speed (15/16 seconds to the furlong), as this promotes relaxation. At this stage the horses are kept one behind the other, but after a short distance they are asked to draw closer together – to begin with say the fifth and sixth horse coming together, then joining the fourth and so on until they are all gathered up together before being urged to quicken their pace. With this system of first relax, second gather together and then quicken, they are usually eager to do so.

The first season

In Britain racing starts in April, when some of the more precocious two-year-olds will be ready to run. If they show signs of an excitable temperament, despite all the gearing towards relaxation in Michael's stables, they may be taken to a local track to get used to the travelling and to have a spin around the course after a meeting.

A two-year-old may be raced up to seven times, but this is the maximum and it will depend on his constitution and temperament whether as much as this is attempted. Some of the immature two-year-olds may not race at all, so their winter programme has to be varied according to the different stages reached.

The easy months

The busy two-year-olds which have done a good deal of work will be 'let down', that is there will be a reduction of energizing food like oats, and of the work they are given. The fillies might go out to grass, but the colts rarely benefit from such sprees. The ladies being more delicate and sensitive benefit from different food, usually needing to put on weight, and the running free helps them to unwind after the rigours of training. The colts however are by nature stronger, better feeders and are less affected by the changes, so they need less unwinding. Being greedy they also tend to put on too much weight if allowed to eat grass freely. This exercise of 'letting down' the two-year-olds is used to achieve both mental and physical benefits, and a good trainer chooses the type of rest which will best suit each horse.

The colts, deprived of their fun out at grass, are kept in easy work, but of a different type to the spring and summer. The emphasis now is on unwinding rather than conditioning and fittening, so they usually spend a good deal of time of the roads and there is very little cantering across the heath. The colts which were not ready for a two-year-old career have to be brought on so that they can compete with their more experienced rivals in the three-year-old season. For them there will be little road work but plenty of canters and occasional gallops.

Conditioning work

By the turn of the year the rest and recuperation is over and the serious business begins. As three-year-olds the horses will be given much more conditioning work – being more mature, a better foundation can be established before the galloping starts. They will have plenty of road work at the walk and trot, and some up-hill work, progressing to the canter as they get fitter (but not the gallop, as the slope will affect their action and is too much of a strain with the added element of speed). On flat ground they will be given progressively more canters and half speed work. This steady build-up enables the horses to withstand the strains of galloping and racing, and helps them through further barriers in terms of speed and staying power. Such conditioning can only be done with the older horses, however; the two-year-olds are not mature enough to stand long hours of work.

Three-year-old season

The horse's racing programme will vary according to its ability. The stars have a set pattern which involves a major race every four to five weeks, allowing them to recover before each major effort. The lesser horses which are involved in handicaps do not enjoy such a leisurely routine. They have to race when the weights, going and courses suit their particular talents; they may have two or three races within a couple of weeks. This is when good conditioning helps, providing the foundation of muscle and fitness to endure such a strain.

FEEDING

It is not work alone which helps horses withstand the rigours of racing. Food is a vital factor, and is probably more important in racing than in any other equestrian sphere. This is because the training of racehorses in comparison to other sports horses is more concerned with the physical well-being of the animal than with developing skills. Racing entails maximizing the efficiency of the body. Feeding provides both energy and the ingredients needed for muscle development, and it determines weight.

Michael weighs all his horses regularly and he has found that there is a correct racing weight for each horse.

Whether a horse is at peak fitness can be judged by the weighing machine, as well as the way the horse looks and works. An interesting point is that when a three-year-old colt starts to get fit it weighs about 40-50 lb (18-23 kg) heavier than at the same time in its previous year, i.e. growth has increased its weight, but when it is fit and ready to run it returns to within 15 lb (7 kg) of its racing weight as a two-year-old. There is very little variance in a horse's racing weight, so this is an excellent way of judging the state of a horse, and warns the trainer to adjust the feed and work if the weight is not as required.

All Michael's horses are weighed just before a race, to make sure that the horse is at peak fitness – its correct racing weight; just after, to judge how much the race took out of the horse and how long it needs before racing again; and between races, to ensure that it is on schedule for being at the correct weight and therefore will be fit in time for the next race.

For the feed to enable a horse achieve the best condition, develop energy and get to its racing weight at the right time, quantities have to be adjusted according to individual requirements and the feeder must therefore know each horse's capacity. In a big racing stable such as Michael's, where there are over one hundred occupants, this can be difficult so his stables are divided into smaller yards each with its own feeder.

Michael's horses receive a maximum of 16 lb of oats a day – any more than this is excess to energy and muscle requirements and does little more than make them fat. The feed is as natural as possible; there are no new types of mixes, just oats and hay of the best possible quality. With such good feed additional vitamins are less necessary, although Michael does use a Vitamin E supplement as this is particularly helpful for muscle repair. Molasses and sugar beet are also given as fit horses on high quantities of oats tend to become finicky feeders and need tasty additions.

FACILITIES

Training racehorses requires expensive facilities. A variety of gallops of up to a mile long and on very good going – old turf, dirt or other artificial surfaces – is needed to get the horses fit and develop their action. These gallops are expensive to lay and to maintain, and with the vulnerability to injury of the very valuable horses which use them, they cannot be second-rate. Consequently much of the training is done where gallops can be shared. In England the main centres are Lambourn and Newmarket, in France, Chantilly, and in America, where the race meetings last a month or more, most of the training is done on the tracks. American trainers base themselves and their horses at a track for the duration of the meeting, then move on to the track where the next meeting is to be staged.

Generally 30 or more horses are needed to make training a commercial success. This will entail providing a similar number of high-class stables and a large staff: a head lad who feeds and oversees the stable, a travelling lad to drive the horsebox and take the horses to the tracks, one lad for every two to three horses, which they groom, ride out and generally look after, and jockeys who both work the horses and ride them on the racetrack.

THE JOCKEY

Although riding skills play a smaller part in the training of racehorses than horses in other disciplines, they are still an aid to everyday work and vital when it comes to the race itself.

A special horse will take 12-13 seconds to cover a furlong, but only if it is kept balanced. This is a jockey's first requirement – that he has balance on a horse. He may not be a stylish rider, but with balance the horses will be able to run for him.

The next asset is sympathetic hands – the ability to establish a feeling with the horse through the reins that the horse does not want to fight. In this way the jockey can get a horse to relax, to wait for him and not waste its energy in pulling.

Hands and balance are natural talents, but as in the other equestrian sports they can be improved with experience and training and will be of use to anyone who wants to ride horses in any sphere. But the other vital requirement for racing is more particular to it, and that is judgement of pace. A jockey to succeed has to know how fast his and the other horses are running. He has to judge the stamina and speed capacity of his horse in relation to the others and to the distance of the race. Then he must decide whether he can let the field go away, content that he will be able to catch them later, or whether they are not going fast enough to test the stamina of his horse so that he has to take the lead. He then has to judge when he should ask his horse for its effort, and must have the strength to be able to do so without losing his balance and interfering with the rhythm of the horse.

Michael, as a racehorse trainer, stays on the ground so he needs a further attribute in his jockeys: they must be able to analyse how the race was run as well as the potential of the horse they were riding, and relate these in an articulate manner to him.

Harness Racing

Ragnar Thorngren

INTRODUCTION

Harness racing is very big business in most countries where horse racing is popular, Britain being the exception. Here the sport is practised only in Wales and the north-west and it has never developed into a national commercial activity. In Europe, North America, Australia and New Zealand there are large numbers of luxurious harness racing tracks, where to add to the spectacle many of the meetings are held at night under floodlights. The prizes are as large as for flat racing, and leading harness horses may win close to a million pounds during their careers. These highly remunerative prizes are possible because harness racing is an excellent betting medium so that huge sums are waged by the punters.

The harness racer pulls a lightweight vehicle with bicycle-like wheels, called a sulky. The driver has a small seat in which he stretches his legs in front of him, his feet secured in metal hoops called stirrups. He needs security for the horses reach terrific speeds. Although not allowed to gallop they are nearly as fast as flat racers. They either trot, in which case the legs move in diagonal pairs, or pace, when the legs move in lateral pairs. The pacers are marginally faster and may average 32 mph (51 kph) over one mile (1.6 km). (The record speed for the greatest flat race, the British Derby, is only just over 35 mph, or 56 kph.) Trotters, although a little slower, reach speeds of over 30 mph (48 kph).

The tracks are usually circular, and vary in standard from temporary grass tracks which are used as part of local annual fairs, to permanent courses with extensive racing facilities rivalling those of the leading flat race tracks.

The range of distances for harness races is not as great as for ridden racing. The majority are run over about a mile, although two-year-olds race over less than this, and the older horses up to two miles.

NATURAL TALENTS

The shape

When inspecting a young horse for the first time the natural features Ragnar Thorngren looks for are an intelligent eye, and ears which point forward and are set far apart on a broad forehead. The nostrils are best if wide. The length of the head should be in harmony with the rest of the body.

The angle of the shoulder should be as close to 45° as possible. A clearly defined wither is important, as is a deep broad chest giving space for the heart and lungs. The forelimbs must be well positioned, and this is only possible if the horse has a broad chest which provides space for the forelegs. In addition the horse must stand correctly so that there is a straight line from the point of the shoulder to the hoof with no sign of the limbs turning out or in. The knee joints should be firm and free from any puffiness. The angle of the pastern should be about 55-60°. The pastern must not, under any circumstances, be too short but if it is long this does not matter (the opposite requirement to polo ponies).

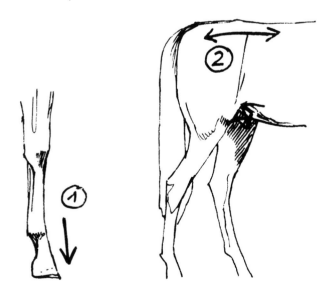

Fig. 72 Conformation defects in a harness horse. (1) shows a very straight pastern, (2) a very straight croup.

The hindquarters of the horse are very important. The slope of the croup should be 10-15°; if it is any flatter this can cause sore muscles. The thigh should be twice the length of the cannon and well covered with muscle. There must be no windgalls or other signs of puffiness. The angle of the hock should be 155-160°. The cannon should be broad and firm and free from any signs of growths. The hooves are important and need to have been well cared for from an early age. A correct hoof should have no rings since these can be signs of potential problems.

It is important to inspect the horse both from the front and the side. The perfect trotter should have harmonious overall proportions, and a useful indication of such harmony is that the height of the horse at the wither is the same as its length from the chest to the hindquarters.

Temperament

The temperament of the horse is important if it is to become a successful harness racer. Ragnar Thorngren likes to see a young horse which is curious and gay, without appearing nervous. Horses that show the white of the eye are often difficult because in general this is a sign of a nervous temperament.

Action

When the young horse moves around the paddock or is lunged one should look for athletic harmonious action with a good length of stride. The head should be held naturally in a good position – neither too high nor too low. It is best if the forelegs move freely and are not hit by the hind legs, although such a problem can sometimes be cured in a young horse by fitting special shoes with carefully adjusted weights.

CHANGES THROUGH TRAINING

Training for harness racing, like flat racing, is geared to make the horse physically fitter and mentally relaxed, while retaining a strong fighting spirit. There is much more scope in harness racing, however, for improving the action. The racing gait is not natural to the horse – although selective breeding is helping to make it more so – therefore a horse has to be taught to go much faster at the trot or pace than it would ever do running free. It has to learn to control the natural tendency to gallop whenever asked to go faster. Through training its two-time gait (pace or trot) can be improved so much that it achieves great speeds at a gait which was meant to be for slower work. The horse is rarely naturally balanced to do this, so training will help to adjust its balance and to develop freedom and speed in the gait.

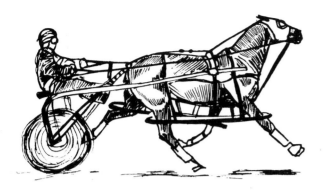

Fig. 73 A pacer moving lateral legs together. It is equipped with hobbles.

Fig. 74 A trotter moving diagonal legs together.

TRAINING

Work from the ground

Each horse is an individual, and young horses do not always behave in an expected pattern. The golden rule for success in teaching the horse to accept being driven is to treat it with a friendly but resolute hand and with a positive frame of mind.

When tying up the horse to put on the harness for the first time it is best to attach rubber bands to the ends of the rope. If it pulls back it will not be frightened by the feeling of a fixed tie rope as the elastic bands will allow some flexibility, and if it breaks away it may simply be tied up again.

Throughout the early training, when the young horse is bound to be scared, time must be taken to stroke and talk to it, and try to develop its trust. It is vital never to be in a hurry with any detail at this stage.

When the horse is sufficiently relaxed for you to consider taking it out, connect two rope lunge-reins on to the bridle. The horse may then be taken for a walk, which should not last more than 30 minutes. On all the early outings a helper must be used. The helper leads the animal by the head while the trainer walks behind teaching it to respond to the rein aids. The work is continued for about two weeks, gradually progressing from mainly straight lines to turns, circles and eventually a left and right volt (6 metre circle). These figures are first done at the walk, but as the horse understands what is required they can be tried at the trot.

Training cart

As soon as the horse becomes obedient and relaxed when driven in long-reins it can be tried in a training cart (also known as a speed cart). The training cart is more comfort-able for the driver and allows him a better view of the action of the horse than the sulky.

The rope reins are changed for leather reins. The cart is brought behind the horse and first the right and then the left shafts pushed alongside the horse to accustom it to their feel. The shafts are moved gently up and down so that the horse understands how close the cart is to it.

Having ensured that the cart is properly fastened, you may ask the horse to move forward with the helper leading its head. To avoid the horse being frightened by the noise of the cart it is a good idea to put some cotton wool in its ears.

The horse is walked for the first couple of days. The trainer must take care not to frighten it or risk the cart hitting an object, so narrow paths should be avoided. After about a week the horse can be driven for fifteen minutes or so, and this can be increased by five minutes per day until it is having sufficient exercise for its state of fitness. Part of the daily work must include teaching the horse to stop and start.

Balancing

When the horse has been driven for a month, the speed at which it works may gradually be increased. After about six months a sulky may be used instead of the training cart, but not more than twice a week.

At this stage a decision may be made as to what balance best suits the horse. The balance is usually adjusted by means of weights varying from 50 to 150 grams (2-5 oz) which are attached to permanent fixtures on the front shoes. These weights are only attached for races or training; if they are not sufficient, shoes made from different materials such as iron, aluminium or plastic, or boots made with rubber or lead can be used.

A pacer racing. Note how the hobbles stop the horse from trotting, as this horse's lateral legs are not moving simultaneously and the straps of the hobbles are taut thus preventing any further disparity.

Another pacer moving out well on a training spin.

The young horse may need quite heavy weights at first. Some rare horses which are naturally highly talented trotters will not need weights, even in the early stages, but most will lack a consistency in action and speed. Weights can be used to correct all these factors. As the horse achieves a better balance, the weights may be reduced; the aim is to make the balancing as light as possible, even to the extent of removing all weights.

Skilful balancing is one of the most important aspects of

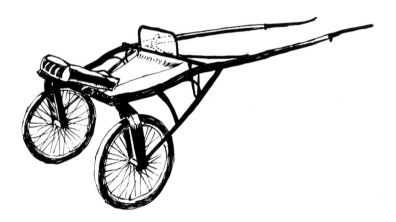

Fig. 75 The sulky, which is used for racing, is designed to enable the horse to go as fast as possible.

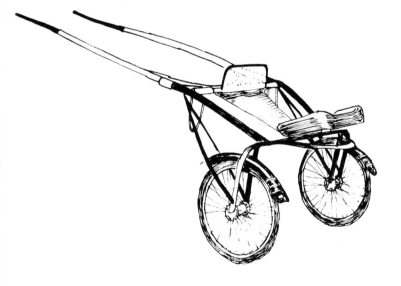

Fig. 76 The training cart is stronger and more comfortable for the driver than the sulky.

harness racing. Although selective breeding is producing more horses which are born with the ability to move in the required manner, it is not natural to trot or pace at high speeds. The weights are necessary to improve the action of the horse, to prevent the legs striking each other at the higher speeds, to encourage the front legs to move faster and more freely and to give more space for the hind legs to run.

Apart from adjusting the weights, balancing is also aided by the shape of the horse's shoes. The shoeing of harness horses is a great art. A far greater range of shoes is used than in any other equestrian sport because they can alter the natural action of the horse thus not only helping it run faster but also reducing the strain placed on the tendons and joints.

'Speeding'

As the young horse progresses the pace can be increased on the days when it is driven in the sulky, and it can be taught to 'speed'. The horse should never be driven alone during these exercises but in the company of other horses, preferably three or four, and the positions with these changed continuously so that it learns to speed equally happily whether on the inside, middle or outside.

Before a harness horse starts racing it is usually given at least 100 training races of a mile (1.6 km) each. Two to three training races can be driven in a training session. On the days when the horse is not driven in training heats it is exercised at least 6 miles (9.6 km) per day.

The races

If there are no problems with this progressive training the horse can start its racing career. In the United States it is usual for horses to begin racing as two-year-olds but in most other countries they begin as three-year-olds.

When the horse is being raced regularly it can exercise itself in the paddock and the training heats may be reduced. This usually results in a happier, more harmonious horse which will do better in races. Ragnar Thorngren likes his horses to have as much time as possible in the paddock, but is careful as to which horses are turned out together, since fights easily lead to injuries.

Harness horses are raced at either the trot or the pace. In Europe the races are for the trotter behind a sulky or ridden (known as *monté* in France). In the United States the horses race behind the sulky at both the trot and the pace, the pacer being more popular because there is less risk of it spoiling its chances through cantering, thus being a safer bet for punters.

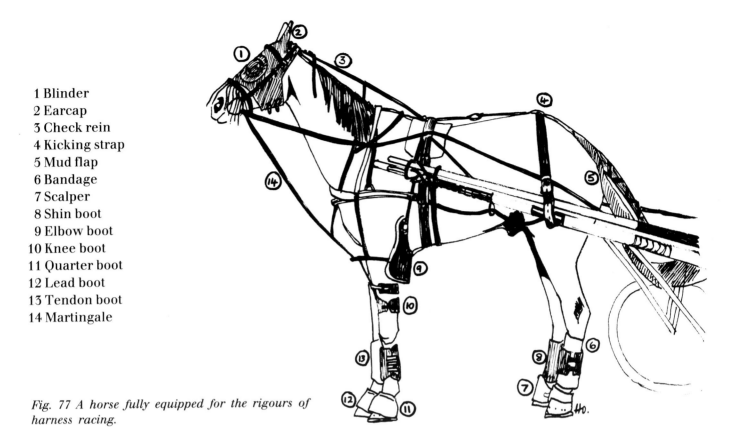

1 Blinder
2 Earcap
3 Check rein
4 Kicking strap
5 Mud flap
6 Bandage
7 Scalper
8 Shin boot
9 Elbow boot
10 Knee boot
11 Quarter boot
12 Lead boot
13 Tendon boot
14 Martingale

Fig. 77 A horse fully equipped for the rigours of harness racing.

The training of trotters and pacers is similar, although the pacer is always trained and raced in hobbles. These are attachments to the legs which stop the horse trotting rather than pacing and help it to keep its balance when pacing at speed. In general it is easier to train a pacer because pacing is not such hard work as trotting and the horse is therefore easier to keep sound and mentally keen. A trotter is more difficult to balance and therefore demands a trainer skilled in this art. It follows that the trotter requires more training before it can start in its first race.

FEEDING

A very important factor in producing a successful harness horse is the feeding of the young animal. From the time it is weaned it should have an abundant supply of first-class hay and fresh water. It should have good chalk-rich paddocks on firm high land, preferably with some hilly woodland for protection. The horse must be given additional food such as oats or maize even when it is on grazing. When it is being worked this hard food must be increased.

When the horse is being raced continuously it is fed largely with hay, oats, bran, molasses and different kinds of mineral food. The mix of the food may be varied depending on each horse's size, temperament and how well it takes to the food.

TIME SCHEDULE

Harness horses can, if they are talented and fast, start competing as two-year-olds. In the United States all horses are trained to start as two-year-olds; in Europe this has been unusual but the current trend is towards the American schedule.

Two-year-old races are run over a mile, whereas older horses compete over distances between 1 and 2½ miles. All races are started with either a mobile starting barrier or with each entry turning in small circles.

The young horse can be entered in Stakes, major races in which a financial stake is paid so that the horse can be entered in selected races during its three- and four-year-old seasons. After the horse has reached the age of five it can compete in different classes depending upon its winnings. A horse's racing career is much longer in harness racing than in flat racing. In Sweden for example stallions can compete until the age of twelve and mares until the age of ten. The demands of this sport are not so great as for other forms of racing.

Western Riding

Sandra Rappaport

INTRODUCTION

The sport of western riding is a direct and recent outgrowth of the working life of American cowboys in the late nineteenth and early twentieth centuries. During the past dozen or so years western riding for fun rather than use has become increasingly standardized, yet its underlying principles as well as its tack and other equipment remain closely linked to the requirements of trail and ranch life. Western criteria for horse and rider, which sometimes contrast sharply with those in other equestrian disciplines, are more understandable when viewed in the context of their origins.

The basic elements of western riding are the paces of walk, jog (slow, smooth trot) and lope (slow, smooth canter). Every western horse also learns to back quickly and obediently: in addition, many are also taught manoeuvres such as the flying lead change, sliding stop, spin, and roll-back (180° turn). After its early education, the horse is then taught either to perform very slowly and smoothly or to move with more speed until it can change pace and direction very quickly and accurately. Whether its eventual training stresses slowness or speed depends on the events for which a horse shows particular aptitude as it progresses.

Despite the adaptation of ideas and methods from dressage by some of its trainers, western riding still diverges from other types of horsemanship in significant ways. Once the horse's training is finished, the rider has

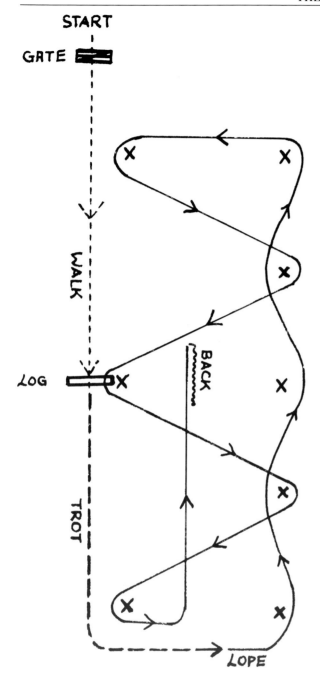

Fig. 78 A typical western riding pattern used to test a horse's ability to act as a good mount on a ranch.

to reduce seat and leg, as well as hand, contact with his mount. An English rider might find communicating with his horse rather awkward under such circumstances, but the accomplished western rider can transmit his wishes so effectively that he controls his horse through all paces and movements, and at all speeds, with signals that are nearly invisible. Achieving this goal requires not only a distinctive approach to training, but a unique sort of horse.

Western riding encompasses a broad range of events, each with its own requirements for the horse. The sport can be roughly divided into 'slow' classes such as western pleasure and western riding where there is greater emphasis on conformation and quality of movement as well as on total compliance with the rider, and 'fast' competitions such as reining or cutting where the horse's execution of a task or pattern weighs more in the balance than its beauty or way of going.

Before it specializes in any branch of western riding the horse must learn walk, jog, lope and backing, and must neck-rein (turning left when the right rein touches its neck, and vice versa). Then it may be trained for one or more of the following.

In western pleasure classes the horse should appear to be 'a pleasure to ride': comfortable at every pace, quietly manoeuvrable within each pace and from one pace to another. The pleasure horse travels on a loose rein yet maintains the slow speeds of perfect control, not varying its head position during upward and downward transitions.

In western riding classes, supposedly judged by the standards for a mount which might carry a person safely and comfortably around a western ranch, each horse and rider perform a test pattern. First there is a gate to be opened, passed through and closed as smoothly as possible; next the horse makes the transition from walk to jog while hopping over a small log. The major part of the test consists of complex serpentines with ten or more flying changes indicated by markers on the course. The horse, whose lope must be a true three-beat pace, should travel straight between the markers and arc through each curve as it turns for the next. This requires balance and suppleness. To excel in western riding the horse must change leads not only with willingness and accuracy, but prettily.

The trail class harks back to cowboy days when a horse might be its rider's sole form of transport across hazardous country. Each horse and rider must negotiate a series of obstacles whose sequence and construction will vary from show to show. (In one class, competitors had to pass between two freshly killed beef carcasses to enter the ring.) The trail class always includes certain objects: a gate which

little direct feel of its mouth because the reins are usually left slack and are both held in one hand. (This practice stems from the working cowboy's need to have one hand always free to use for tasks such as handling a lasso or opening a gate.) The western rider sits with his legs almost straight, in a saddle whose clearance above the animal's back (accentuated by a double-thick pad) is greater than that of a forward or balanced seat style. These factors tend

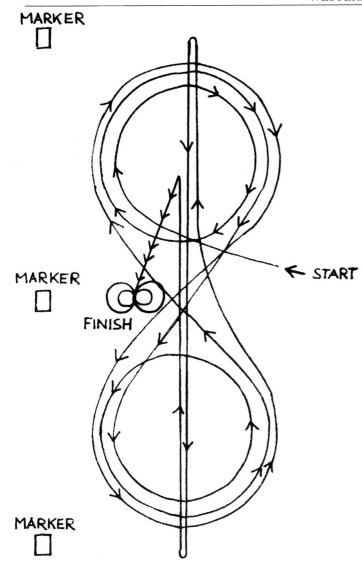

MARKER ☐

MARKER ☐

FINISH

← START

MARKER ☐

Fig. 79 A reining pattern which has to be completed at speed, testing the horse's agility and ability to accelerate and stop quickly.

the rider must unlatch, pass through and refasten by means of side-passing and backing without having to dismount; a wooden bridge; and at least four logs which the horse must step over. Other common tasks are an L-shaped backing pattern and a series of automobile tyres into whose centres the horse must step. As a test of its attention to the rider, the trail horse might be required to step gently over a raised pole and then jump a pole laid flat on the ground. A good trail class ride is a smoothly integrated performance, not a series of jerky stops and starts.

Reining is a fast event. Like those just described it emphasizes rider control of the horse's movements, but at working rather than pleasure speeds. The reining test will be one of several standard combinations of large circles ridden at gallop, small circles at lope, flying lead changes, roll-backs, spins, sliding stops after maximum straight-line acceleration, and fast back-ups. The horse executes this pattern on a loose rein in response to indirect neck-rein, shifts of the rider's weight, and voice commands.

In cutting competition, which is another type of fast work, the horse is awarded points for its ability to separate a cow from the herd, bring it under control, and manoeuvre it along a fence line – all with minimal guidance from the rider. Working cow horse trials combine reining and cutting skills, requiring the horse to perform a type of reining pattern (called 'dry work') in addition to the cow work.

There are other cow events in which western horses compete with the more active partnership of their riders. These include calf roping, team steer roping and steer wrestling.

NATURAL TALENTS

The modern western horse rarely exceeds 16 hands, though a deep-girthed body makes it a comfortable mount for a big man who would feel under-mounted on a light hunter of the same height. Western conformation seeks to combine substance with style: a sturdy body with a sprinter's short bunchy muscles (rather than the long flat musculature of a distance runner) tapers off into clean straight legs proportionately shorter than a thoroughbred's and a pleasing head with a small muzzle and large eye.

In order to respond well to the western rider's subtle signals the horse must be very sensitive, but without the excitability which sometimes accompanies sensitivity in other breeds.

In its way of going, the horse which is a natural choice for western riding has smooth paces. The rider can sit comfortably and quietly to its jog without posting. It covers ground with minimum knee and hock action (in contrast to a dressage horse) and tends to carry its head and neck in a relaxed, outstretched position as it moves.

The western horse is famous for its capacity to accelerate to top speed over a short distance, though it can sustain the sprint for only a limited time. Originally an asset in chasing wayward cattle, this talent for quick bursts of speed also proved useful for sport. The Quarter Horse was so named because of the breed's historical supremacy in informal quarter-mile flat races, and many still compete in that event at recognized tracks.

Since the western horse has a compact build, it is also very handy at abrupt stops and quick changes of direction.

Trail. Patty Knudson is taking her horse over a bridge with tyres. The horse must stay on the bridge and step over the tyres without knocking them off or hesitating.

Left: Cutting. Note the horse's attentive expression, focused on the cow. This natural involvement is called being 'cowy' and it is the quality a trainer requires in a young horse if it is to be successful at cutting.

These abilities are important in the day-to-day business of working cattle, and are also prerequisites for some popular show competitions.

The innate athletic talent of the western horse is coupled with a tractable temperament which suits it to this riding style, for western riding demands more complete mental as well as physical submission, and a higher level of performance at an earlier age, than most equestrian activities. The horse with a passive and even temperament can more easily adjust to the pressures of a training schedule where it is broken to saddle at the age of two and may compete at major events well before its third birthday. Rather than developing or preserving the horse's spirit which is the aim in other equestrian sports, a western rider seeks to make it surrender its will readily. The only part of its personality the western horse is encouraged to assert is 'cowy-ness', an interest in cows and a knack for anticipating their evasions, which is essential for success in the specialized event of cutting.

Specialized talents

Each category of western riding, slow and fast, emphasizes different aspects of the natural horse and also makes its own demands for change in the horse. Advanced training for slow classes enhances the western horse's natural softness and the low action of its paces while seeking to establish even rhythm and greatly reduced speed at the jog and lope. A horse that is naturally supple will be encouraged in the tendency for slow classes until it 'follows its nose around' when asked for a change in direction; this contributes to a soft, easy look. The horse that does well in the pleasure class must also carry itself naturally in a balanced frame without too much weight on its forehand. Training then reinforces this quality until ultimately the horse remains 'backed off the bridle' at all times, balancing itself without seeking the rider's hand. This way of going also helps the horse to balance itself through the turns and lead changes of western riding with barely perceptible cues from the rider.

Fig. 80 The pleasure frame. This horse has been trained to adopt this outline, also known as 'Texas style head position'.

Notice how far above its back the thick pad and large saddle place the rider.

A note on western style collection: English riders describe a horse as 'collected' when it is compressed between the rider's hands and legs with its haunches engaged, and moves with higher, rounder strides in a shortened frame. The collected western horse must also shift its weight to the haunches and move from behind; however, its stride remains low and quiet, nor does it 'fill up the reins' and communicate with its rider through the bit as an English horse can. One mark of collection in western riding is the horse's ability to perform a true jog and lope very slowly, and to change paces with minimal head motion, but the horse is taught to balance itself in this way while staying 'backed off the bridle' so that the reins remain slack. In the increasingly popular style of western pleasure riding termed the 'California look' or 'California head-set', the horse learns to carry its head in the nearly vertical position typical of a dressage horse, but does so while working on a loose rein.

In contrast with the classes which emphasize softness and slowness, reining and cutting events require that trainers bring out the western horse's free forward movement, combining extreme manoeuvrability with speed. For fast events the horse carries its head and neck in a level, natural position and, unlike the supple pleasure horse, the reining or cutting horse is encouraged to keep its body as straight as possible at all times as an aid to achieving correct stops and spins. This focus on straightness includes teaching the horse to gallop a circle not by following the circle's arc of circumference with its body but by holding its body tangent to that arc and staying on the curve by crossing over with its front legs. Horses do not advance far in these events unless they have natural aptitude for the spin and the sliding stop, which are then quickened until they become a blur of movement. Another important element of reining and cutting, though it comes naturally to only a few horses, is the rapid back-up. This movement is usually performed at trotting speed, immediately after the sliding stop in the reining test; again, this is easier for the horse that has learned to hold its body straight.

Many top trainers feel that although nothing prevents an athletic horse from performing well in both slow and fast events, the two fields of effort make opposing demands. Therefore, the more advanced the level of competition becomes the more likely that the horse will have to specialize in one category or the other. However, with proper retraining it is possible for a western horse to specialize in one type of event for a while and then switch to the other.

Fig. 81 The 'Californian head set'. The horse's head is vertical yet the reins are still loose.

TRAINING

In the earliest days of western riding, unbroken horses were often roped, restrained, forcibly saddled, and ridden until resistance ceased – all in an afternoon. Their subsequent training in the finer points of cowboy work was on the job.

Today's western horse is brought along by far gentler means. The schedule for western training, however, is still compressed in comparison to that for a dressage or event prospect which will not be expected to reach the height of its powers until years after training begins. The western horse matures a little earlier than some other breeds, and there is strong emphasis on young horses in western competition. Futurity classes are an important goal for two-year-old pleasure prospects and three-year-old reining and cutting horses. By the age of five or six, when many combined training mounts and jumpers are just becoming serious contenders, a successful western horse may well have left the upper levels of showing to become a youth or amateur horse or to be used for breeding.

Obedience

Whatever the western horse's career is to be, its initial training includes certain key elements. Its obedience to cues (aids) which will eventually become very subtle

Reining. This is a spin turn used in reining patterns. The aim is that the inside hind foot should remain planted while the right hind steps around it.

A well turned out rider for a western pleasure class. It is important that the outfit should tone in – the hat, with the chaps, with the vest (waistcoat).

begins with learned responses to strong, obvious signals which grow lighter as understanding develops. The young horse is taught either to hold its body straight (for reining and cutting) or to 'give its head' and arc in the direction indicated by the rider (for slow classes).

The western trainer then wants to gain control of the horse's action components – head, shoulders, and haunches – so that he can refine its movements. He wants its head position consistent through changes of pace and speed, its shoulders level during turns, and its haunches well under its body so that its weight stays off the forehand and out of the bridle.

Work from the ground

Basic training for the western horse can begin at weaning time when it is a few months old. After separation from its dam the young horse is halter-broken and learns to obey voice commands from the ground. During this time 'Walk', 'Trot' and 'Whoa' are associated in the horse's mind with a cluck of encouragement, or with gentle restraining pressure from the halter noseband.

Schooling then stops until the western horse is about two years old, which is the time for saddle breaking. The western saddle is large and relatively heavy; with its wide skirts it touches a considerable area of the horse's back. All trainers take great care in putting on and taking off the saddle during the first few days, and in addition some 'sack out' the young horse, rubbing it all over with feed sacks to accustom it to the touch and proximity of large flapping objects.

The next step is working the saddled two-year-old from the ground, either on the lunge or at liberty, while it adjusts to feeling the saddle on its back as it moves. The round pen, which has about the radius of a lunge line, is often used for this stage. There the trainer can use voice commands which the horse learned during halter breaking, with signals from a lunge or buggy whip, to ask for walk, jog, lope and halt in each direction. Some trainers will also encourage the young horse working at liberty to execute a simple roll-back from a halt at this time, as a way of evaluating its balance and way of going.

Mounted work

Round pen work continues for two or three weeks, until the young horse is confident and relaxed. When mounted work begins, it is with a continuation of the cues to which the horse has already learned to respond. Instead of a bridle, for the first ridden work it wears either a light rope hackamore with rings to attach the reins at either side of the muzzle, or a bosal with the reins attached to a knot under the chin.

The trainer wants the two-year-old to learn to move away from leg pressure, but he begins by asking for walk, trot or lope with voice cues or clucks and uses his leg simultaneously until the signals become associated. When asking for a halt he says 'Whoa' and bumps the horse's nose with pressure on the reins as he used to with the halter lead shank. And although he will eventually hold the reins in one hand and guide the horse with a touch of the outside rein on its neck, at this stage he 'plow-reins' by holding one rein in each hand like an English rider so that he can tug the nose the way he wants it to go. Once the horse is responding to a direct rein, the trainer can teach it to neck-rein by simultaneously giving a direct cue with the inside rein and, with his other hand, laying the outside rein against the horse's neck.

After a few weeks of training in the hackamore or bosal, the western horse is fitted with its first bit. This is not the curb which most will wear later on, but a simple ring snaffle which may be added to the headgear already in place by means of a separate crownpiece. Often the trainer leaves the reins attached to the noseband for a few days while the horse adjusts to holding the bit in its mouth, then adds another set of reins so that he can ride with both noseband and bit. When the horse accepts pressure on the bit rather than on the hackamore or bosal for stopping, turning and backing, it can progress to a regular snaffle bridle. At this point, ridden work has usually been going on for about two months.

Tackling resistances

Every western trainer has favourite techniques for overcoming the evasions and resistances which inevitably crop up in young horses during these weeks. Rather than simply intensifying a signal which is not working, he will often deal with the problem by substituting a different and rather more direct signal.

For instance, when the horse balks at backing from gentle pressure on the noseband or snaffle combined with an encouraging cluck and a backward shift of the rider's weight, the trainer may slap its shoulders lightly with his feet as an added cue – something which the long western stirrups allow him to do easily. A foot-slap may also be used on the inside shoulder as a reminder to the horse to balance itself if it is sinking the shoulder on a circle. Another correction for balance on the circle is counter-cantering or, if the problem is caused by over-bending, a direct outside rein to decrease the arc of the horse's body.

Even if the horse has advanced to neck-reining, its trainer will revert to a plow-rein whenever he feels the more subtle indirect cue failing to convey his message.

Circles

Circles are an important training tool in establishing the speeds of western paces, especially the lope. Rather than increasing pressure on the reins when a young horse wants to go too fast, the trainer can ride it into a smaller (hence more difficult) circle which forces it to slow down. Eventually the horse adjusts its notion of what speed is acceptable without feeling it has been punished.

Head position

Quiet head position is essential in most western competitions, and is achieved in part through prevention: the horse's gradual introduction to the western curb bit by way of the hackamore and snaffle keeps him from fearing it. The horse which still persists in flipping or bobbing its head may give up the habit if the trainer moves his hand counter to the head motion so that its resulting discomfort to the horse is exaggerated. When the head is quiet, the trainer holds his hand still as a reward.

Correct lead

In correcting a young horse which tends to pick up the wrong lead at the lope, some trainers seek to increase its responsiveness to leg cues by asking it to side-pass in one direction, then signalling it to pick up the lead in the opposite direction. A horse that is bent slightly to the left for a side-pass to the right will have its body well positioned to pick up a left lead. Or the trainer might reinforce the cue for lope by swinging his inside leg towards the horse's shoulder so that its inside hind leg is freed to move further forward for an energetic departure.

Changing the balance

A western horse which is heavy on its forehand cannot sustain the balance and drive needed for true paces at slow speeds or for rapid changes in direction. An English rider trying to shift his horse's centre of balance rearwards will often ride it forward into the bridle; by contrast, the western trainer whose horse is lugging on its forehand will halt and back for a few steps as a correction. Backing strengthens and increases the suppleness of the horse's back and hindquarters, and brings its hind legs underneath it. From the back-up the trainer might ask his horse to move directly into a jog, watching to see if its head remains quiet in order to gauge whether it has collected itself. By

repeating this correction whenever the horse becomes too heavy in the bridle and does not respond to the lightest of rein cues, the trainer encourages it to stay 'backed off the bridle' without having to exert continuous pressure on its mouth.

Specialization

By the time the horse is consistent in all three paces, backs readily with a lowered head, responds to neck-reining cues, and can keep its body balanced through changes of pace and direction, it is ready to specialize in the type of western riding for which it is most suitable.

In evaluating a young horse for pleasure classes, the trainer looks for the best possible conformation, including an elegant head whose profile is straight or, preferably, slightly dished. As well as being balanced enough to travel in a pleasure frame, the horse should have paces so soft and light that it appears just to 'sneak along the rail'.

An attractive western horse whose gaits are not quite low and smooth enough for top pleasure classes may be a candidate for western riding if it has a pretty and well-balanced lope. A horse may also excel in trail without exaggeratedly slow and perfect gaits; in addition, trail classes permit (sometimes even require) more head movement because the horse is expected to look new obstacles over carefully as it proceeds. The trail horse must be handy in movements such as side-passing, backing, turns on the forehand and haunches, and negotiating low jumps.

Western horsemen feel that it is now often necessary to have a horse that is good looking as well as athletic to succeed in the cow-orientated classes such as cutting and reining, but the horse which does well here must above all have the 'sting' which shows that it enjoys its work.

THE TIME SCHEDULE

Basic training for the western horse, beginning with saddle breaking and ground work when it is a long yearling or short two-year-old, will take about three months. During this time it will work five or six days each week for thirty to forty-five minutes per day, with time off whenever it appears tired and a return to earlier, easier work if it seems confused. The pleasure prospect is then polished in its paces and frame for a few more weeks, perhaps with an eye to showing in one of the highly competitive Pleasure Futurities to which two-year-olds are nominated at great expense. As a three-year-old the pleasure horse is eligible for the Pleasure Maturities.

The reining or cutting horse which has completed the

Teaching a young horse to spin. Al Dunning has rocked his weight back and is not putting much pressure on the horse. He 'plow-reins', holding one rein in each hand so that he can flex the nose in the direction required. When the horse responds well to the direct rein it is then taught to neck-rein.

basic training outlined above can learn the elements of its event in three to four months more, but will then need several additional months to master and perfect them. Reining Futurities are for three-year-olds, Maturities for four-year-olds, and the most spectacular performances are often seen in the open reining classes for horses of five years old and upwards. Cutting and working cow horses are often trained for over a year before competing and may begin showing in a hackamore rather than a bridle if they are under four years old.

There is no seasonal work schedule for western show horses as there is for field hunters or combined training horses. Western riding is more comparable to show jumping in that it continues all the year round, sometimes indoors and sometimes outside.

FEEDING

Because western horses are smaller and less highly strung than those used for many equestrian sports, they require comparatively less concentrated feed than other breeds. Western show standards demand that a horse looks well filled out and shiny; beyond that, its diet is determined by the type of events in which it competes. Many trainers favour a traditional combination of oats and hay for western horses, although in some areas (particularly the western United States) there is more reliance on complete pelleted rations.

In conjunction with feeding, physical conditioning is accomplished in the course of the training itself. Work under saddle accelerates muscular development so that a young horse looks considerably more mature after a few months of riding. Some trainers recommend special exercises for a horse which is slow to fill out in one spot; for instance, if the muscles over the loins appear underdeveloped the trainer might back the horse uphill as part of its daily regimen.

EQUIPMENT

Western riding is set apart from all other equestrian sports by its tack and clothing. While horses equipped for the very different sports of polo, dressage and show jumping might appear somewhat alike to the casual observer, the western horse and its rider are unlikely to be assigned to any discipline but their own.

The western saddle, though it may appear cumbersome, was actually developed to be as easy as possible on both horse and rider during day-long use. Its wide skirts distribute its weight and that of the rider over a larger portion of the horse's back than English-style saddles do, while the design of its tree keeps pressure off the spine and loins. Its high horned pommel once provided a snubbing post for bringing a roped cow up short (and still serves this purpose in roping classes), while the raised cantle behind him kept the working cowboy securely in position. Older western saddles tended to tilt the rider slightly backwards so that he was braced between stirrup and cantle, but more modern designs allow him to sit upright and bring his legs directly under him in a western version of the balance seat. The western saddle is held in place by a cord girth with a plain metal ring or a buckle at each end, and for cutting, roping and other working events a flank girth is added further back to keep the saddle from flipping forward under stress. The stirrups, which are adjusted to a length which allows the rider's crotch to clear the saddle if he stands, are roomy and made of lightweight wood. The leathers often include a fender, or wide flap which lies between the rider's leg and the horse's side as protection from the animal's sweat.

The western bridle differs from the English type in a number of ways. It has no cavesson; in fact, nosebands are not allowed in the ring for many classes. (Exceptions to this are the horse that is being shown in a hackamore or bosal, and the working horse that wears a tiedown for strenuous events such as roping.) The most popular style of western bridle is the 'one-ear' type: instead of a brow-band attached to the crownpiece, it features a crownpiece divided at the poll and rejoined near one eye so that it slips snugly around one ear. This uncluttered look makes the most of an attractive head. Since snaffle bits are considered no more than an early stage in the western horse's training, when western riders speak of 'the bridle' they mean one with a western curb bit. These are used alone, unlike the English curb which can be used with a snaffle to form a double bridle. They range in severity from a low port and short shank to the harsh spade which, despite its potential for abuse, can be a humane tool for sensitive control in the hands of a good rider.

The reins may be split so that, if dropped, they fall to the ground on each side of the horse's neck. Western horses were traditionally trained to stand as if tethered when this happened; called 'ground tying', it meant that the rider who needed to leave his horse in a hurry would find it waiting when he returned. An alternative to split reins is the romal, where the ends of the reins are fastened together ornamentally into a long switch. When using a romal the rider holds this end piece in his free hand, and may use it as an aid to his horse.

Fig. 82 The western rider correctly attired and sitting in a good position. The reins of the western bridle are joined in a romal, a decorative endpiece.

The western rider's attire, like his horse's tack, is historically rooted in function. A wide-brimmed hat, tailored shirt, leather or suede chaps, highly tailored pants and heeled boots are standard western wear; the outfit may also include a neckscarf and waistcoat. In the cowboy era a wide-brimmed hat was shelter from sun and rain, chaps shielded the legs from thorny underbrush, and the boots, while supporting the lower legs and ankles, kept the feet from sliding through the stirrups during rough action. A scarf was often tied over nose and mouth to filter out the dust of the dry western climate.

Today, western clothing for pleasure and other slow classes is carefully chosen with an eye to flattering the horse's colour and the rider's physique, while tack may be elaborately inlaid with silver or decorated with carving. For the working events, tack and dress are plainer but must still be neat and workmanlike.

FACILITIES

The facilities needed to train the western horse are relatively simple. Initial halter-breaking and leading often take place right in the reassuring environment of the foal's stall or the barn aisle. Later when it is time for round pen work, the enclosure can be of permanent and durable fencing or a temporary barrier. Once the trainer has equipped the horse with steering and brakes, he may elect to continue working in a confined area where the novice already feels secure. Or, especially in the case of the young horse which seems destined for reining and cutting, he may venture into the countryside where open space encourages free forward movement and obstacles such as fence lines become training aids in teaching straight back-ups and roll-backs.

When the horse is ready for more specialized work, an enclosed arena with good footing is important for teaching the elements of reining. The cutting horse, in addition, will eventually need real cows on which to practise – it should begin by working around calm, passive animals and progress to trickier and more aggressive ones as its skill develops.

The trainer preparing a horse for trail classes needs to approximate as many as possible of the problems which the horse might face in competition. Any fenced area can serve as a practice arena, with an array of obstacles built from common materials such as tyres, pylons, rails and jump standards.

THE RIDER

The western rider functions without the close contact with his horse on which the English rider depends. In its place he uses position, posture and feel to help maintain communication. The good western rider has a natural inclination to sit *down* in the saddle, allowing his legs to hang at the horse's sides; there should be no tensing of the thighs or gripping with the knees. With this relaxed seat, which instructors say is one of the most difficult things to instil by teaching where it does not exist, the rider needs good posture so that his shoulders, hips and feet are vertically aligned regardless of the pace at which his horse is working.

Correct position and posture are the prerequisites for 'feel', a sense of what the horse is doing or is about to do with its body. Relaxed and in place, the rider can learn to distinguish whether his horse is properly balanced and moving from behind. He can make slight corrections before problems develop. Feel is to some extent an inborn ability but it can also be developed through appropriate instruction and the opportunity to ride many different horses.

Despite the wide range of events which western riding embraces, few riders or trainers are specialists in a single field. The western horse is versatile; so is its rider. But whether jogging sedately on the rail in a crowded pleasure class or galloping into an empty arena to begin a reining pattern, the rider must convey the confidence and trust in his horse that is the foundation of his sport.

Barrel racing. This shows the moment in the turn when the horse must hug the barrel while remaining balanced and able to push out of the turn into the next straight.

Training a pleasure horse. Jody Gallyean using the side pass to help make his horse more supple, and to move off his leg. He is bending the horse around the leg he is using to move it sideways.

GLOSSARY

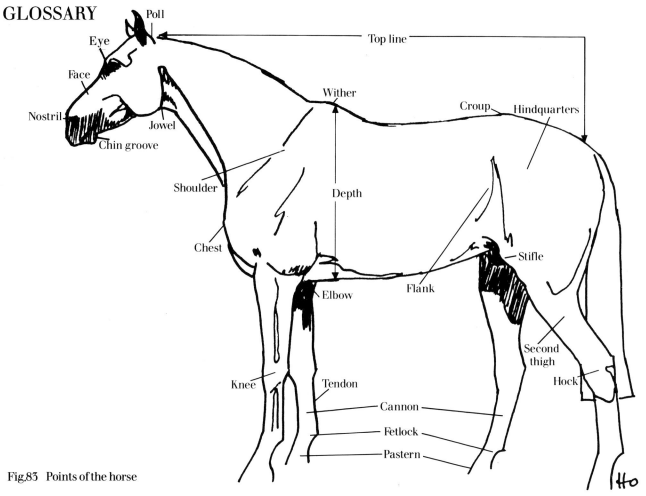

Fig. 83 Points of the horse

AIDS Signals whereby the rider conveys his wishes to his horse. The natural aids are the voice, hands, seat and legs. The artificial aids are the stick and the spur.

ARC The bend of the horse in western riding.

BASCULE A well-rounded (convex) top line in jumping. The horse drops its head and neck at the summit of the obstacle and its back is convex rather than hollow.

BOSAL A bitless bridle of rope or rawhide in which the reins converge to a knot under the jaw. Pressure is exerted on the bony part of the nose and under the chin.

BONE A measurement of the circumference of the bone immediately below the knee. A horse with good bone (i.e. large circumference) is capable of carrying a heavier rider than one that is light of bone.

BOUNCE The horse takes no stride between two obstacles but has to land and immediately take off again for the next fence.

BRIDLED Trained to respond to the rider's cues while keeping a proper head position on a loose rein.

CADENCE Term used to describe gaits and paces which have a pronounced rhythm. With cadence the rhythm has energy, which gives more bounce to the strides derived from a marked flexion of the joints and engaging of the hindquarters.

CANNON *See* Fig. 83

CHUKKER A period of play in polo lasting seven minutes. A game usually consists of six chukkers, although there may be eight.

CLASS Term used to define a highly refined horse with great stamina. The good thoroughbred is said to have 'class'.

CLASSIC Non-handicap races for the best three-year-olds. These are the most prestigious races. In England they are the Guineas, the Derby, the Oaks and the St Leger; in the USA the Kentucky Derby, Preakness Stakes and Belmont Stakes.

COLDBLOOD A heavy horse used for industrial and agricultural work or transportation.

COLLECTION A state in which the horse's body has been compressed so that the strides are short and high, the hindquarters are low and the hind legs move well underneath the horse. The opposite state is extension.

CONFORMATION The make and shape of a horse. A horse with poor conformation has weaknesses in certain areas which will limit its athletic ability and make it more susceptible to lameness.

CROSS BREEDING Breeding from two horses of different breeds.

CROUP *See* Fig. 83

CUES Western term for aids.

DISHING When one or both forelegs are thrown out to the side instead of the leg or legs going straight forward.

DOMODOR Argentinian gaucho specializing in the training of polo ponies.

DOUBLE BRIDLE A complete snaffle bridle plus an extra headpiece, cheek pieces, pair of reins and a bit with a curb chain. The rider controls the horse with two reins, the snaffle rein being the mildest. The horse has two bits in its mouth.

ELEVATION A good spring to the stride.

EXTENSION The longest possible strides, the opposite to collection.

FETLOCK *See* Fig. 83

FLYING CHANGE In the canter the horse leads with either the near (left) foreleg or the off (right) foreleg. To change leads the horse may be brought back to the trot or walk and given the aids for the opposite lead, or if it is sufficiently trained it is asked to change leads during the moment of suspension in the sequence of the canter.

FOREHAND The front section of the horse – the forelegs, shoulder, neck and head. A horse is said to be on its forehand when it is carrying a relatively high proportion of its weight with its forehand rather than hindquarters. This makes it less mobile, and less able to spring into the air.

GAG Type of bit in which rein pressure is applied not only in the mouth but also in the corners of the mouth and on the poll. It is a severe bit.

GAITS (also known as paces) The normal gaits are walk, trot, canter and gallop.

GRID A series of small fences placed at calculated distances from each other so that the horse can either bounce between them or take one or two strides.

HACKAMORE A bitless bridle which acts on the nose and chin. The reins fasten to the sides of the muzzle, not underneath.

HALF PASS A dressage movement in which the horse moves forwards and sideways. The horse is slightly bent in the direction to which it is moving. The forehand is slightly in advance of the hindquarters but the body is as near as possible parallel to the long side of the arena or school.

HAND Unit of measurement (4 inches, 10.2 cm) of the height of the horse from the wither to the ground. A horse is said to be so many hands high, abbreviated as 'hh'.

HARD FOOD The higher energizing feeds such as oats (most important), barley, maize and so on, as opposed to

hay and grass which is known as bulk feed.

HOBBLES Straps used in harness racing to stop a pacer from trotting. They connect the foreleg to the hindleg on the same side, thus inducing the legs to move in lateral pairs as in pacing, rather than diagonal pairs as in trotting.

HOCK *See* Fig. 83

IN-BREEDING The mating of brother and sister, sire and daughter, son and dam.

JOG A slow smooth trot in western riding.

JOWEL *See* Fig. 83

LASSO A long rope tied into a loop at the end, used in catching cattle.

LINE-BREEDING The mating of horses which have one or more common ancestors, but some generations removed.

LONG-REINING Controlling the horse from the ground by means of long-reins attached to the bit.

LOPE A slow, smooth canter in western riding.

LUNGING A long rein (lunge-rein) is attached to a cavesson (a padded, tightly fitting form of headcollar) or to the bit of the bridle and the horse performs circles around the trainer who stands in the centre holding this rein.

MOUTHING BIT A bit used in the very early stages of training. It is usually straight (no joints), and may have holes in it or keys attached which encourage the horse to play with them with a relaxed jaw and not to grip tensely to the bit.

NECK-REINING The horse is asked to turn by the rider placing both reins in the direction in which it is desired to turn the horse rather than by pulling on the rein or reins on the particular side (direct reining or plow-reining).

ON THE BIT The position of the horse's head at which the rider can most easily exercise control. When the horse is on the bit the poll is the highest point, the face of the horse is close to the vertical and it is accepting happily the contact with the rider through the reins; the hindquarters are well engaged with the hind legs well under the body. When the head is too high the horse is said to be above the bit and when too low and close to the horse's chest it is said to be behind the bit or overbent.

OUT-CROSSING The use of outside blood in breeding.

PACE The same as gait, but may also be used to refer to a variation of the two-time gait of the horse when the legs move in lateral pairs instead of diagonal pairs as in the trot.

PASSAGE A very highly collected, elevated and cadenced trot in dressage. There is a longer moment of suspension than for any other form of the trot.

PASTERN *See* Fig. 83

PELHAM A bit with a curb chain. When rein pressure is applied it will be felt by the horse in the mouth and also along the groove of the jaw just above the lower lip, where the curb chain runs.

PEN A riding ring in western riding.

PIAFFE A highly collected, elevated and cadenced trot on the spot, demanded in the most advanced dressage tests.

PIROUETTE A circle performed in dressage on two tracks with a radius equal to the length of the horse, the forehand moving around the hindquarters. It can be performed in walk or canter: at the walk it is usual to be a half pirouette, and in the canter the half pirouette is used in the earlier stages of training.

PLEASURE FRAME The carriage of the trained western pleasure horse, when it shows the correct head position, with slow paces and engagement of the hindquarters.

PLOW REIN The term in western riding for using a direct rein which is applied with one rein in each hand. In western riding neck-reining is the ultimate aim.

POLL See Fig. 83

PORT An indentation in the centre of the mouthpiece of a bit which gives the horse room to move its tongue.

PRESENCE A quality possessed by certain horses, consisting of an alertness and an air which draws the eye to such horses.

REBENKE A short stick with a flap on the end used in the Argentinian method of training polo ponies.

REIN BACK The backward movement of the horse through pressure on the reins. In dressage the horse should raise and set down its legs in almost simultaneous diagonal pairs, each foreleg being raised and set down just before the corresponding diagonal hind leg.

ROLLBACK A change of direction in western riding in which the horse plants its inside hind foot while the forelegs push its body through a 180° turn.

ROMAL A variation on the western bridle. The reins are sewn round and joined behind the horse's withers into a decorative endpiece.

SEQUENCE OF GAITS/PACES At each gait there is a correct sequence of footfalls. At the walk four hoofbeats should be heard at equal intervals; the order is left hind leg, left foreleg, right hind leg and right foreleg. At the trot two hoofbeats should be heard; the legs move in alternate diagonal pairs separated by a moment of suspension. At the canter three hoofbeats are heard, followed by a moment of suspension. The order of legs will depend upon which leg is leading: with the left foreleg leading the right hind would be followed by the left hind and right foreleg together, then the left foreleg before the moment of suspension. At the gallop four hoofbeats should be heard followed by a moment of suspension; with the left foreleg leading the

sequence is right hind leg, left hind leg, right foreleg, left foreleg, followed by a moment of suspension.

SHOULDER-IN A lateral dressage movement in which the horse moves at an angle of about 30° to the direction of the movement, with the horse bent slightly around the rider's inside leg and away from the direction in which it is moving. The horse's inside foreleg passes and crosses in front of the outside leg; the inside hind leg is placed in front of the outside leg.

SICKLE HOCK A weak hock which is bent, resembling the shape of a sickle.

SNAFFLE BIT A mouthpiece, which may or may not be jointed, attached to rings on either side. There is no curb chain.

SNAFFLE BRIDLE A bridle with a snaffle bit attached.

SPIN A reining and cutting movement in western riding in which the horse plants its inside hind foot and pivots rapidly through several complete turns by stepping sideways with the front legs.

SPOOK Nervousness displayed by stopping, shying or snorting when seeing something.

STANDING BACK Taking off a long way back from a fence.

STIFLE See Fig. 83

SULKY The racing cart used in harness racing.

THROUGH An expression used in training to describe a horse which is working without resistance. All the muscles have tone and are not stiff, and the hindquarters are co-ordinated with the forehand so there are no 'blocks' in the system. In such a state the horse's strides will appear to have spring and the back will be supple and will swing (shown by a slight swing to the tail).

TIEDOWN The western variation of the standing martingale which is attached to the noseband for strenuous events such as roping.

TRACE Part of the harness which attaches the horse to the carriage.

TRAVERS A dressage movement in which the horse is slightly bent around the inside leg of the rider and positioned at an angle of about 30° to the line of the track it is following.

WARMBLOOD The breed of horses with studbooks which lie between and have often been the result of crosses between the coldbloods (q.v.) and the hotbloods (Arabs and thoroughbreds). These are the breeds which are used for equestrian sports other than flatracing.

WHEELERS The horses harnessed behind the leaders and in front of the carriage.

WHIP The person who drives the carriage.

WITHER See Fig. 83

INDEX